TEN TAYSIDE DOCTORS

TEN
TAYSIDE
DOCTORS

J. S. G. BLAIR

1990

SCOTTISH ACADEMIC PRESS
EDINBURGH

Published by
Scottish Academic Press Ltd.
139 Leith Walk
Edinburgh EH6 8NS

SBN 7073 0600 0

British Library Cataloguing in Publication Data
Ten Tayside Doctors.
  1. Scotland. Doctors—Biographies
  I. Title
  610.6952092

  ISBN 0–7073–0600–0

Printed in Great Britain by Bell and Bain Ltd., Glasgow

TEN TAYSIDE DOCTORS

Acknowledgements

Introduction

Acknowledgements

I wish to thank the relatives of the doctors, and some of the doctors themselves, for their help in supplying me with factual material of their lives and work. I would also like to thank very much those who have read and approved the accounts. My thanks also go to Mrs Joan Auld, archivist at Dundee University, for help in supplying information and photographs, to Mr Lewis Robertson for his helpful information and comment on events during his period as member and later Chairman of the Eastern Regional Hospital Board, and to Mrs Valerie Pringle for typing the manuscript.

I have also to thank Professor K. G. Lowe for advice and support, the Carnegie Trust of Scotland and the Guthrie Trust of the Scottish Society of the History of Medicine for considering the work appropriate for grants by them, and the kind friends who contributed towards the cost of publication of this book.

Introduction

'Let us now praise famous men' said the writer of the Ecclesiasticus in the *Apocrypha:*

> The heroes of our nation's history,
> Some held sway over kingdoms
> and made themselves a name by their exploits.
> Some led the people by their counsels
> and by their knowledge at the nation's law;
> out of their fund of wisdom they gave us instruction.
> Some were composers of music or writers of poetry ...

But, he goes on

> There are others who are unremembered;
> They are dead, and it is as though they had never existed,
> as though they had never been born
> or left children to succeed them ...

describing the great mass of humanity, referring to our own selves.

Yet, says the preacher

'a few have left a name behind them to be commemorated in story'.

Our ten doctors are just such—nine men and one woman. Their only common thread is the River Tay. All of them lived much of their medical lives near or actually within sight and sound of that great Scottish river, and their places of work extend from its upper reaches to its estuary.

The Tay rises on the north side of Ben Lui 3708 feet above sea level. To Loch Tay it takes 25 miles to flow, and the loch itself extends a further 14 miles to Kenmore. In another 14 miles, it meets the Tummel. From that junction to the city of Perth, before the doubtful regionalisation of the 1970s when it lost its Lord Provost the second city to Edinburgh in Scottish historical status, is some 30 miles, and from Perth to its mouth beyond the city of Dundee is about another 30. It is one of the great rivers of our land.

But the population is sparse in the upper miles of its course, and so most of our doctors did their work between the cities of Perth and Dundee, where the people who needed their services lived. We have a doctor from Aberfeldy, one from Crieff and later Bridge of Earn; a physician from Perth and a practitioner from Newburgh. *He* was made a freeman of that town—the greatest public honour of them all. Next we have a surgeon who lived at Invergowrie in a house called Tayside, but whose work was in Monifieth and Perth. From Dundee, as befits our greatest town we have four doctors, including our lady, and lastly, to complete our number, a practitioner from Newport and Ferry-Port-on-Craig.

These ten are representative of the multitude of doctors whose lives are lived and whose contributions made in places far from the famous centres of the world, where there was little or no likelihood of any great gifts they might have or devoted care they might give being ever widely known. Their grateful patients would as often as not die before them. Their small obituaries would be unread except by relatives or their friends. Especially if the only recollections others had of them were as elderly or even infirm, their 'years of youth and high powers' would in the same way be unknown to successors.

None is a university professor—though more than one could have been one if they had so decided. None is a national name, poet, musician, soldier, politician governmental or medical, whose record of honour, painting or statue was commissioned by a grateful nation. Some had happiness and success but some knew failure, mental agony and some the bitterness of enduring that delight a few doctors take in attacking their colleagues. Because their lives are mainly in the present century, parts of these were spent in foreign fields in great wars; these very testing times added an extra dimension to their experience and so to their patient care after their return. Their variety of interest is great, their range of activities fascinating, their abilities undoubted. Their life stories call for commemoration:

Let us now praise these famous men.

Walter Walker Yellowlees

Walter Walker Yellowlees,

MC, MB, ChB(Edin), FRCGP

At Aberfeldy the Tay is already a grand river. The townspeople enjoy its fresh waters as they flow by, and the historic Wade's bridge is the window you look through towards the lovely routes to Weem and then to Fortingall and Glen Lyon or to the north shore of Loch Tay—both to the west, or to Coshieville, Tummel and Rannoch—to the north. These are some of the most beautiful parts of Scotland.

From Aberfeldy comes Watty Yellowlees, as all his friends call him, the first of our Tayside doctors. His background and his forebears are typical of a professional man of his walk of life—how much happier is that Scottish expression than the English equivalent of 'social class'!

He was born in Stirling in 1917, where his father's father had been provost. His father had trained as a ship's engineer but was offered, and accepted, the post of joint Managing Director of Stoddart's carpet factory at Elderslie in Renfrewshire. So the family moved there in 1919. His mother was a daughter of the manse; her father was a Rev Robert Primrose, a famous minister of the kirk in his day. Watty was the middle of three brothers, and the family was a close and very happy one. Their home at Elderslie, although it was beside the factory, stood by the Brandy Burn flowing down from the Gleniffer Braes of Renfrewshire, and

I

was in a country setting. From their early days the boys enjoyed the countryside and all the outdoor activity that went with it.

Their education was at boarding schools—first Hurst Grange Preparatory School in Stirling, then at Merchiston Castle School in Edinburgh. Watty was not enthusiastic about leaving home for school but 'I suppose I was saved' as he once said 'by being reasonably competent at games'. This was a typical understatement. He was an outstanding games player—captain of his school rugby 1st XV, and a member of both the 1st rugby XV and the 1st cricket XI, when he later went to Edinburgh University, from 1937–40. In the 1939–40 season he was captain of both teams.

As well as being good at team games, he was an athlete of note, and was President of the Athletic Club in Edinburgh in 1940–41, his final year in medicine. He met a number of people in these years whose influence moulded many of the attitudes he grew into in later life.

The most important of these was Colonel H. B. Campbell, head of the University Physical Education Department. He was an enthusiast and a visionary. When war broke out in September 1939 he organized work camps for students in their vacations. Watty went to one of these in the Borders, and was impressed at Colonel Campbell's commitment. He helped to organize a Boys' Club in Glasgow and in 1941 one of these clubs went to Argyll to work on Watty's older brother Robin's farm at Strachur.

Robin was a powerful character with wide interests. He rented Strachurmore Farm—it was a sheep farm of Cheviot sheep with a dairy herd as well. During his own university vacations Watty and his younger brother Dave went to work on the farm—the work was very hard, as men were in short supply and the hours long. It was then that Watty became interested in nutrition, while feeding his brother's farm livestock. Robin did not stay in his reserved occupation but joined the RAF. He was tragically killed while training in 1940, just after he had got his wings.

2

Never distinguished academically, his liking for medicine was 'strong enough for me to manage to surmount professional examinations without repeats'. He qualified in 1941, worked for a couple of months as Assistant in the Venereal Diseases Department in the Royal Infirmary of Edinburgh, and returned to Stirling in October to be House Surgeon to Mr George Reid's wards until April 1942.

War Service came next. After his basic training with Scottish and Northern Irish RAMC Lieutenants at Beckett's Park in Leeds, he was posted to 220 Field Ambulance then stationed in the North Riding of Yorkshire. Let him tell of his next two years in his own words:

'In October '42 we embarked as 9 Corps Field Ambulance with the Anglo-American invasion of North Africa. The convoy sailed from the Clyde. It was a huge affair and I don't think any ships were lost until we came to the North African coast, and were discovered by German and Italian bombers. Our Field Ambulance landed with the troops who had been allocated to the small port of Bougie near the Tunisian border. When we eventually joined hands with the Eighth Army at the final battle for Tunis and Bizerta I asked for a transfer to the 51st Highland Division and was posted to 152 Brigade Field Ambulance, which with the Division was getting ready to invade Sicily. (Their General, Douglas Wimberley, was adept at encouraging Scotsmen to join his splendid Division, but Captain Yellowlees' request for transfer was his own). About the second day after landing our Brigade was heading the advance with the 5th Camerons the leading battalion. The Camerons met fairly stiff resistance from the German Hermann Goering Paratroop Regiment. Both the Cameron CO and their Medical Officer a Captain Montgomery were wounded ... as the most recent arrival with the Field Ambulance I was detailed to go and take the place of the wounded MO. I stayed with the 5th Battalion of the Camerons during the Sicilian campaign. We did not go on to Italy but came back to the U.K.

3

in the autumn of 1943. We were to be part of Monty's Normandy invasion and spent the winter of '43–'44 training, based in Surrey. We landed at Sword Beach in Normandy on D plus 1, (D-Day was the first day of the invasion, D+1 the next, and so on) and took over from the paratroopers of the 6th Airborne Division who had captured Pegasus Bridge and the bridge-head beyond it on the East side of the Caen Canal. Until the breakout in July '44, life around Caen was really pretty unpleasant. It was explained to us that our role was to attract as much of the German might as possible to our part of the line, while the Americans swept around the right flank (which they eventually did)'. Dr Yellowlees then added, as an afterthought 'I was awarded the MC in the Battle for the village of St Honorine'.

Captain W. W. Yellowlees was in fact an outstanding Regimental Medical Officer. The history of the Scots' contribution to Military Medicine is a long and distinguished one, from James Lind the father of Naval—and all other—Preventive Medicine, Sir John Pringle the epidemiologist to the European wars of the mid-eighteenth century who anticipated bacterial contagion as the cause of wound infection, John Hunter the scientific observer of wounds, Sir James McGrigor the Aberdeen Director General and devisor of the principles of military casualty evacuation, the 'great named' Generals and Admirals, to the humble Regimental Medical Officers. Study of history shows that the humble earned deeper love and reverence than the greater.

Watty Yellowlees was one of these. He was remembered for ever by members of the 5th Bn, the Queen's Own Cameron Highlanders, as *their* revered medical officer. So great was his reputation that he was recalled by Major-General Wimberley to medical cadets in St Andrews OTC, after the war, as an example of the best sort of regimental medical officer, one they should be proud to try to emulate.

In 1946 he was demobilised. At first he went back to Stirling, to the Royal Infirmary there to train as a surgical registrar. But the

4

discords he found in hospital quietly decided him that hospital medicine was not to be his career, and he 'set about finding jobs which would fit me for general practice'. He studied obstetrics in Dumfries, did a house physician's job at Perth Royal Infirmary, and followed that by a paediatrician's job at the Western General Hospital in Edinburgh. While he was in Perth he heard that Dr Jack Swanson of Aberfeldy was looking for a partner. He visited Aberfeldy in April of 1948 to see if he could obtain the assistantship. He did, and stayed in Aberfeldy for the next 33 years.

In 1948 also he read Lady Eve Balfour's book *The Living Soil*. This told him of the researches of Sir Robert McCarrison on nutrition and health. The interest stirred in him by his dearly loved elder brother Robin about the effect of diet and the soil on health was re-awakened. McCarrison's work was a revelation to him, and gave for him a view of health and disease much wider than had been dreamed of in university departments. Dr Yellowlees had observed at once that the beautiful and tranquil upper Tay valley gave no immunity from the degenerative diseases of the big cities of civilisation. The researches of Sir Robert in India seemed to explain why—the people of this part of Tayside were for the most part eating a diet exactly as he had demonstrated—a diet associated with degenerative diseases and infection. It was lacking in vitamins, minerals, fibre and perhaps other as yet unknown factors in fresh whole food. It was loaded with refined starch and sugar. The book *The Saccharine Disease*, by T. L. Cleave, also took his interest, and greatly influenced him also: he called it 'a milestone' after he had read and re-read it. And so, rather like Sir James McKenzie of a half century earlier, he set out to study the natural history of disease in his country practice and see how it related to the nutrition and habits of the inhabitants. Like McKenzie, he was many years ahead of his time.

There was more to practice in rural Tayside than the study and recording of nutrition and disease. But his study *was* of interest; the recent war had as one of its bonuses produced food rationing, which ensured a fair distribution of dietary necessities—something that had not existed in British society before 1939. In and around Aberfeldy there were extra items available than in the big cities— more milk, butter, fish and meat. But of the food available, only vegetables and a little fruit were grown in local soil—and by no means the majority. The changes from locally-grown food to 'imported' processed products began as long before as 1840, and was hastened by the coming of the railway in 1867. Work was outdoor, slums and factories absent. Agricultural workers were poorer than many realised, but they still had access to some extras in diet, and still enjoyed traditional fibre in the form of porridge. Yet there remained 'plenty of disease'.

The practice was a very good one. As well as being a man who reached high office in British Medical Association Councils, Dr Jack Swanson was a diligent and careful doctor. He was a good obstetrician. But he did not believe in careful written recording. By contrast, no matter how busy he was on BMA business—and he was *very* often in Edinburgh or London, he always made time to write, in his neat hand, letters of thanks and acknowledgement to hospital and other colleagues. It was old-style courtesy. Watty Yellowlees had this careful concern already—aware of the need for written accurate records—and he developed it over his years of service in the town. He gave patients time. He made early use of the laboratory facilities being offered to practitioners in Perth Royal Infirmary under the new National Health Service. The recently appointed pathologist there, Dr John Prain, though gruff at times, was excellent at encouraging doctors from city and county to use his facilities—especially the developing ones for chemical testing of blood and tissue fluids. Over the years, hospital doctors came to recognize his neat small handwriting, referring a patient for opinion or admission as an emergency. The percipient (and the seniors were all percipient) got to know that if *that* was Dr Yellowlees' diagnosis, then *that* was almost certainly correct.

6

During the early, happy years of the NHS, when the need to pay the doctor seemed to have gone for ever, and poor people especially in the large towns no longer delayed calling the doctor for fear of being unable to pay, he did an immense amount of work. From about 1953 till 1958 the presence of 600–700 hydro-electric construction workers living in hutted camps in Glen Lyon added greatly to the practice work load. The local women, men, and children of the upper reaches of the Tay were not demanding, querulous, or hypochondriacal. If they called the doctor they needed his services. As everwhere they had their share of mentally ill, socially unstable, and downright wicked individuals. All were given the doctor's time. He served loyally, too, as an elder of the Kirk, and brought the faith he had re-gained in the hard times of the war from the Cameron's padre to the help of many.

Because Aberfeldy was so isolated, and nearly 30 miles from the nearest large Infirmary, it had its own cottage hospital with its own maternity. It had its own X-ray apparatus, and the two local doctors took X-rays and acted upon them. 'Did you ever set fractures?' Dr Yellowlees was asked. 'We weren't supposed to, but we did—wrist and ankle ones that were straightforward'. It was entirely reasonable especially as his first house post in Mr Reid's wards in Stirling had included orthopaedics, and he had done orthopaedic training as a surgical registrar. And then, of course, he had his wealth of war-time experience packed into those few eventful years.

Surgery apart from small lumps and bumps done by the local doctors was never practised at Aberfeldy, but the maternity unit more than made up for this in its activity. Because of Dr Swanson's special interest in obstetrics, Aberfeldy became the 'obstetric unit' for northern Perthshire. Patients were referred from Rannoch and even Pitlochry. During the '50s and early '60s, 120 mothers were often delivered in a year at Aberfeldy, and intervention done when needed, one of the doctors applying the forceps and the other giving the anaesthetic. There was much

7

pressure on the maternity at the Royal Infirmary in Perth in those years, in its still quite limited accommodation, and Miss Elliot and later Mr Ian Fraser were glad that some was relieved by the skill and safety of the Aberfeldy doctors.

In 1950 Watty married Sonia, the daughter of J. H. Doggart, FRCS, the London ophthalmologist. He worked at several of the London hospitals including the Sick Children's at Great Ormond Street and was the author of a standard text-book on Diseases of the Eye in children. Their children were Robin, Michael and Jane. Michael took ill with acute appendicitis in 1966, and Watty took him to Perth where a newly-appointed surgeon had recently started work. Much to the alarm of the younger man, Dr Yellowlees, by now a senior doctor of note in the county, came into the operating theatre to watch him remove the boy's perforated appendix.

Before the General Practice Reforms of 1965 Sonia Yellowlees was closely involved in the running of the practice—answering the door bell (for their house was the surgery) and the telephone. The extra dimension in rural practice was the remoteness of many patients—some lived thirty miles from the doctor's house, and many farms could only be reached by very rough roads. 'So without the help of our wives' said Watty twenty years later, 'Jack Swanson and I would have found it difficult to endure the very heavy load, before we could take a third partner and the reforms of 1965 helped us to set up centralised consulting and start an appointments system'.

Aberfeldy was not all work and no play, however. Watty Yellowlees played cricket for Stirling County when he returned after the War, and for Perth County during the eight months he was in Perth. Soon after going to Aberfeldy he found cricket enthusiasts in the town and in 1949 he helped to revive the Breadalbane Cricket Club. He even organised the laying of a new square for cricket in the Victoria Park; the Breadalbane Club still flourishes.

8

In 1948 began his association with nutrition and soil. He joined the Soil Association, attended its meetings and after consultation with other doctors and dentists of like interest, he initiated the McCarrison Society: he chaired the meeting in the Ivanhoe hotel in London in 1960 at which its formation was agreed unanimously by those present. He continued as President for several years. Support was poor among the bulk of the profession until meetings held in London and Oxford showed increasing attention being paid to the Society's aims and recommendations. In 1976 membership was extended to dieticians and other allied sciences; there is now a regional group in Scotland and the north west of England based in Liverpool.

This interest turned him into an advocate of organic farming many years before its necessity became accepted by a wider public. For many years very many doctors and dentists regarded the McCarrison Society as a collection of cranks; time and experience are now vindicating the Society's views. McCarrison's experiments with laboratory animals had seemed to show that grain grown with the use of cattle manure had a higher nutritive value than that grown with soluble chemicals. Over the years Watty Yellowlees experimented with various ways of growing his own vegetables using organic methods. In 1978 he was rewarded by being asked to give The Sir James McKenzie lecture in London ('Ill fares the land') on the subject—now *his* subject—of 'Nutrition and Health'. Ten years later these views are increasingly accepted by a steadily enlarging number of the population both at home and world-wide. Watty was indeed a prophet whose preaching is now bearing fruit.

Yet doctoring and the care of his patients remained his major life's work. He was a founder member of the Royal College of General Practitioners in 1954 and was Provost of the East of Scotland Faculty in his town. He was a regular commissioned contributor to the Rural Diary in the Faculty Bulletin. He produced teaching tapes for the College, some of which are unsurpassed, both in their content and in their artistic excellence.

For his work, his observations, his careful recording, his energy, Watty Yellowlees deserves a place beside the nationally famous Dr William Pickles of Yorkshire and his classic short book *Epidemiology in a Country Practice*. It was a great loss that he did not begin to make his 30 years of observation and conclusion into a book until his retiral. But now his contribution is recorded and its worth assured.

When he retired in 1981, the first of our 10 doctors opened a small pottery in the town where he had given his life-time of service. Some years previously he had begun to take evening art and pottery classes at Breadalbane Academy. The pottery he made was of professional standard—another immense skill he characteristically, as always, dismissed almost shyly. His show room, in a former garage across the street from the surgery, is now a thriving Art and Craft Gallery. He continued to go down to Perth for BMA meetings, and his opinion on medical problems of the hour was always worth listening to. He enjoyed good health— he was a solid advertisement for his dietary principles. He grew organic vegetables and experimented with crops, in his own garden. Like the old soldier of Classical Rome, he had earned his reward and an assured place in Perthshire's medical Hall of Fame.

Harry Allan Graham

Harry Allan Graham

BSc, MD(St Andrews), FRCSEd, 1900–1989

Our next doctor went with the century. His father was the RSM of the Black Watch in Perth and he was born in that city. When his father retired, he went to Dunfermline as custodian of King Robert's great abbey, so Harry grew up there. At Dunfermline High School he was dux and an outstanding athlete.

But in 1917 there was only one avenue for a young man to follow. So as soon as he had taken his Higher Leaving Certificate, he joined the Royal Flying Corps. He had 60 hours of flying training, and then 10 hours only of flying the Sopwith Camel, the front-line aircraft of the day, before being posted to France to active service with 505 squadron at Arras. He recalled how very thorough their training nevertheless was. 'We had engines, rigging, armament–the whole works of an officer's life. We had to have the RFC manual by heart'.

'When I watched that TV programme called "Dawn Patrol"' said Harry, 'I was very indignant. It said the pilot's life expectancy was only five weeks. And then I realised I was only a month in Arras, as I only got there in October 1918!'

He flew sorties and saw action. His propeller tip broke off when he crash landed one day. 'There were no concrete runways, of course. So if you were taxi-ing in and hit a soggy bit, your nose tipped down and your propeller broke off'. Like others he had his propeller tip, made beautifully of a blend of African walnut and

African mahogany, made into an ornament, with his photograph in RFC uniform above it.

After the Armistice Harry Graham, with hundreds of thousands of others, was demobilised and returned home. He wanted to study medicine, and his hope was Edinburgh University, still the first choice of the majority of Perth school-leavers. 'I thought all I had to do was send my Leaving Certificate to Edinburgh and I'd get in' he said. But he found there were many others in the queue for Edinburgh medicine before him, and was told that the waiting list for admission there was two years. So he thought of trying aero-engineering, to make use of his war training and experience. Then his father met Dr Dow of Dunfermline, a member of the University Court of St Andrews, and Dr Dow wrote on Harry's behalf to 'Andreas' Bennett, the University Secretary, who replied by letter 'there is a place for you'. This was in late September 1919, a year after the war had ended.

His year was a small one in numbers, the complete medical school at St Andrews having only been fully functional since 1895. But in his time there he got to know Sir Stewart Duke-Elder and Sir Benjamin Rycroft, the ophthalmic surgeons, and Sir James Webster, Sir Bernard Spilsbury's successor as Home Office pathologist, two of them senior to Harry, Rycroft a contemporary. But 'the best man in my year' he recalled 'was Henry Scrimgeour. He took all the medals. He went into the Malayan Medical Service, survived the war, retired and came back as an assistant senior administrative medical officer at the Regional Board—of all things'. Surprisingly often—or perhaps not surprisingly often—the contemporaries who became great names in the public world were not those necessarily remembered with the greatest respect and affection by their fellow-students.

Harry Graham was captured by the old grey town as so many before and since. Professor Waterston in Anatomy, and the greatly-loved Professor Herring in Physiology, were the medical professors. But the person he remembered most was Professor

James Irvine FRS the brilliant carbohydrate chemist, who would become Principal and Vice-Chancellor in 1921. He remembered the day the Principal-elect walked into his chemistry class, and amid cheers promised to give his life to their University. In those years a keen sportsman, Irvine played tennis and went swimming with the students—as did Professor Herring—'and Harry Graham as captain of the University rugby team had a great deal to do with him. He remembered the new Principal attending a rugby club dinner where the speaker, a rugby international, could not attend at the last minute because of illness. Harry Graham asked him if he would mind saying a few words, and he responded with an eloquent, rousing speech. He complimented 'J.C.I.' after the dinner, when the Principal replied 'I always take a prepared speech with me to any dinner I'm invited to'.

Clinical years in Dundee involved moving there to student digs but a few students remained in St Andrews until the last possible moment, travelling daily by train until their final year. Harry Graham was one of those, both because he enjoyed St Andrews so much but also because of his rugby club activity. His stay there was longer than average, because he also took a BSc in 1923 before his MB ChB in 1925. In his final year, he was asked by Professor Jock Anderson to be his house surgeon 'because I was captain of the rugby team' he recalled laughingly. There began a friendship which continued until Professor Anderson's sad and early death.

The Infirmary was busy and the work hard. The long, open, Nightingale wards were filled every 3 days with emergencies. If all the beds were full, extra beds were brought in and placed in a line in the middle of the ward. There was no time off. All case sheets had to be complete by the next morning's ward round. The house surgeon on arrival was presented with an open razor by the hospital barber which was his for the 6 months of his housemanship. It was his job to shave the skin of all male patients before their operations. And if this was not enough, the house surgeon had also to give anaesthetics to all emergency cases. The 'honorary' anaesthetists of the day did no emergencies, no matter how ill the patient. This added a great deal of responsibility to a young doctor, but most managed to survive if all their patients did not.

Some housemen took to giving anaesthetics better than others and Dr Graham was one of these. Professor J. A. C. Kynoch, the Professor of Obstetrics and now an old man with a tremor of his hand, came in one evening to do a caesarian section. As his houseman was away, Harry was called over to the maternity ward to do the needful. Afterwards, he walked back with the doctor who had sent the patient in, to his car on the front park of D.R.I. The next afternoon Professor Anderson told Harry that the doctor, Dr Alex Stewart of Crieff, had telephoned him to say 'I liked that young man. Would he come to Crieff as my assistant and then come into my practice'. The professor's word was enough, and Harry found himself in Crieff; such was appointment to general practice in the 1920s!

Crieff suited Harry well, as it had a thriving cottage hospital where he could do what surgery he felt was in his capacity. He went for a year as assistant—in 1926. He became a partner in September 1927. The next year Dr Stewart—who though only 63 years old was universally known as 'old Dr Stewart'—died, and he took over the practice. Doctoring in the Crieff area meant harder work, longer hours, and greater obstetrical and surgical drama than is imaginable nowadays. 'Medical' drama was less striking, since so little could be done for so many medical diseases and patients could only be helplessly watched as they died.

A good number of Perthshire patients were wealthy, and demanded long hours of attention. One such lady became pregnant after several years of marriage, and engaged a Glasgow obstetrician to look after her at her confinement. What antenatal care there was—and this was not very much—was given mainly by her own practitioner. The great man saw her two or three times.

When she went into labour, Harry telephoned him, and relayed progress by telephone. Things looked a trifle slow. He 'phoned again for advice, and was told to inject pitocin, a drug which increased uterine contraction. Her uterus then ruptured.

Dundee was much closer than Glasgow, so he contacted Professor Anderson. 'I'll come straight away' he said. 'I'll bring my own anaesthetist, as I'll need you to assist, and I'll bring my instruments, so you won't need to borrow from the Cottage Hospital. Oh, and by the way, my chauffeur's blood group makes him a universal donor. So I'll bring a transfusion apparatus as well and he can give her a pint of blood'.

The operation was carried out with the speed of the surgeons of the day. The baby had died, and Professor Anderson felt it necessary to do a hysterectomy. A direct cross-match of the patient's blood and the chauffeur's, on the back of a white saucer, showed no dangerous agglutination, so a pint of blood was duly transfused. The lady survived, but Harry had to live in the house for a month and two nurses for two months, till she was pronounced convalescent.

A happier result pleased a millionaire from the Glasgow area whose cottage was a few miles from Crieff. His wife had two daughers, and he longed for a son. If his wife's menstrual period was 24 hours late, he would 'phone Dr Graham at once. 1931 saw the discovery of a test of urine which showed whether a woman was pregnant or not, and this man's wife was the first patient of the practice to have it. It became positive one day, a nurse was engaged at once, and the pregnancy ran an uneventful course culminating in the safe delivery of a fine baby boy.

Was all medicine of those days primitive? This *very* remarkable man Dr Harry Graham proved it was not. When in later years— 40 years later—young practitioners or pleased hospital staff listened with a touch of indulgence to 'old Harry' recounting his experiences and giving his opinions formed after so many years of experience at Perth B.M.A. meetings, they were certainly unaware that not only had he written a thesis from his Crieff general practice days, in 1938, but that it had been awarded a gold medal. Its title was *The influence of Vitamin C on the alkali reserve and the oxygen content of the blood.*

The story of his research shows just what a clever, determined and truly remarkable man he was. In 1937 he had the idea of estimating the amount of vitamin C in the urine of his patients, and monitoring its level in those of different age, constitution, and diet. He had read of a method measuring this vitamin which he thought he would try, and he 'rigged up a room in Ivy Lodge (his house) as a lab'. He bought large jars to contain the urine specimens—all urine passed in a period of 24 hours—day and overnight—had to be collected.

After studying vitamin C levels in urine, and showing how little or greatly it varied under different conditions of diet, age, illness, or activity, he decided he would have to extend his research to the estimate of vitamin C in the blood. Professor Adam Patrick came sometimes to Crieff in consultation, and he encouraged the young local doctor. He sent him to Professor Cappell, Professor of Pathology in St Andrews. Cappell was unhelpful and a little dismissive so Adam Patrick put him in touch with Professor Garry, the active and generous Professor of Physiology, at University College Dundee. Once more Graham's personality—open and engaging—won over the professor. Apparatus was obtained, bench space provided in the Physiology Department, and the project jumped from its early beginnings to a much more sophisticated investigation. When the thesis was sent in, and the clinical examination for the MD passed, Professor Patrick told Dr and Mrs Graham that it was to be accepted. But it was only on his hour of graduation that he learned he had been awarded Honours and a Gold Medal—a great feat indeed.

In the clinical practice of the late 1930s Harry Graham expanded his repertoire of surgery at Crieff—his partner Dr Boyd giving the anaesthetics. These were happy years, with an assured status, a healthy family growing up, and the pleasant Perthshire countryside as a background for well-earned relaxation. But the war was approaching. Harry had been the founder and chairman of the British Legion in Perth since 1938—he was an ex-serviceman. In August, 1939, he went to RAF Leuchars to do refresher training, and on 26 August, while on holiday at Elie, a priority letter arrived from the Air Ministry, ordering him to proceed immediately to Uxbridge. Dr Boyd joined the RNVR and he too went to war.

The Second War was as different as could be from the First. After doing batches of aircrew medicals at Uxbridge he moved around a succession of stations—Bournemouth, Skegness, and Melksham in Wiltshire, as physician. He was posted in 1941 to West Africa—much against his will—to be Senior Medical Officer at a 400-bed hospital at Takoradi in the Gold Coast (Ghana). This was a staging post for fighter aircraft, brought by sea from the U.K. home base, un-crated, and then flown in 400-mile stages by pilots who had also come out by ship. Eventually the planes and their pilots reached the North African battlefield. The post was responsible and busy—especially before mepacrine became available for the adequate prevention of malaria. He ended the war as Wing Commander commanding the RAF Hospital at Wilmslow near Manchester, with a mention in despatches, and the air efficiency award.

Back to Crieff in 1945, he left in 1947. He felt he wanted something different, like so many returned ex-servicemen. Surgery had always attracted him since his days with Jock Anderson, and to give himself time for study and income to live on he took the Regional Medical Officer's job in Dundee. In 1949 he passed the examination for the Fellowship of the Royal College of Surgeons of Edinburgh—then a single examination—at his first attempt. Now he could look for a challenging job for a doctor with general, RAF, and surgical experience, at the age of 49.

Crieff had been in Perthshire but not actually on the Tay. At

19

B

Bridge of Earn, in sight of the junction of Earn and Tay, a large Emergency Service Hospital had been built early in the War. Originally meant, like the 'prefabs' of civilian homes, to be taken down at the end of hostilities in Europe, it would last for over 50 years, and become one of the biggest orthopaedic units in the whole of the United Kingdom. In the late 1940s, it was being developed for Tayside especially as an orthopaedic hospital, but would also have general medical, surgical, gynaecological, eye, and ear, nose and throat wards, TB beds, and a large new block situated on its own to be called 'The Fitness Centre'.

The concept of Fitness Centre was a war-time one, born of the need to teach wounded to make themselves fit enough to return to duty, but also to nurse more seriously disabled back to a reasonable life of activity. The Centre at Bridge of Earn was to take not only ex-service disabled, but also provide places for Fife coal miners, then a large force. So its Director would have to be a man of unusual talents to do the job well.

Dr H. A. Graham MD, FRCS, was appointed Director in 1952. 'My post', he said many years later, 'was the subject of concern. And I was the subject of concern'. Yet he was well suited. His war-time experience of returning sick and injured to duty was considerable. His general practice gave him knowledge of the patient's needs within his family and within his home. His academic qualifications were outstanding. His referees were the Director General of the RAF Medical Services, Air Marshal Sir Harold Whittingham, and his number two, Sir William Tyrrel. These two were at daggers drawn in their service, and a contemporary said of Wing Commander Graham that he was an unusual man who could find favour with both of them. The Senior Orthopaedic Surgeon recently appointed at Bridge of Earn, Mr Ian Smillie, told him that he would support him—Smillie had had no service experience, but had worked at Larbert during the war as surgeon to the orthopaedic service there.

Yet his years at Bridge of Earn Hospital were not always happy ones. His unit was a large one—at its busiest receiving patients from as far north as Inverness and as far west as Glasgow. His energy and humanity had huge scope in the job. But he found from an early date that the unit was regarded as fair game for pillage—items small and large—even weighing machines—were taken from it by staff in the main hospital. He initially asked help from the orthopaedic staff in consultation and arranged a regular visit by them every Thursday. But he was upset to find harsh and unfair criticism levelled at him by this department, and he eventually refused to continue the Thursday consultation clinics with it. Though many were frightened of the orthopaedic surgeons, Harry was not.

He retired in 1965—the normal retiral age. Now he moved from Tayside to quite another life, to quite another world. He went as a ship's surgeon to New Zealand where one of his daughers was living, for a short spell. He next went to Pakistan, to a mission hospital at Jalalpur. The surgeon in charge—an eye specialist— was a Dutchman Dr Jan Bakker. Harry had to learn eye surgery, and Dr Bakker taught him to do cataract removals. The general surgery he could do already. On the staff was a nursing sister from Glasgow, and a 'semi-trained' Pakistani nurse who had undergone training in anaesthesia. The hospital had 250 beds, 30 for ophthalmic patients.

The working day began at 6 a.m. Cataract surgery was done in the cooler hours till 8. Twelve patients sat in a row along the wall of the waiting area. They had cocaine drops put in their eyes by a trained assistant, and the surgeon then went to each, injecting local anaesthetic under the orbit. Even after practice, Harry Graham could only remove eight in an hour—while the Dutch doctor ('a beautiful operator' said his Tayside friend) could remove twelve. So 20 patients were operated on in a morning. The patients remained in hospital for a week, then went home.

Breakfast was a 8.30. From 9 till half past 11 was the crowded outpatient clinic—of the sort seen in all Third World countries.

Between 11.30 and 1 o'clock were ward rounds. Later in the day he did his general surgery—amputation of neglected burnt or fractured limbs, hernias, drainage of septic bones or soft tissue abscesses, as well as abdominal surgery. 'We saw no appendix cases'. Much of the anaesthesia was given by the surgeon himself—by spinal anaesthetic. But their native anaesthetist was skilled and safe enough to deal with abdominal cases. In the year he worked in Pakistan he carried out 1,000 operations. He was in sympathy with the Christian mission work and truly enjoyed it; his final week in Jalalpur was spoiled by his falling and fracturing his hip. But with his usual resilience, he recovered quickly.

Everyone yearns for retirement by the age of 60 nowadays, and the tragedy of the 1990s was the disenchantment of so many doctors with the medicine they had once loved so much. The repeated cuts in resources—reductions in hospital beds, nurses, and money for equipment of the 1980s, together with the appearance of 'managers'—both 'nurse managers', 'unit general' and 'general managers', who worked from their offices and whose pay bonuses were related to the amount of money they were able to save, made hospital doctors unhappy and nurses bewildered. The general practitioners felt the squeeze of commercialisation later, in 1989 and onwards. But at 70, Dr Graham was still full of activities and clinical enterprise, and he did locums in the Perth area until his 80's—and with success.

Finally, infirmity began to dog him—his eyesight began to fail. Yet his lovely sense of humour and fun, his clear intelligence, his remarkable memory, and his wise counsel, remained available for all who had the humility to sit by him and to listen. Especially his family—his four daughters, 12 grandchildren, and 11 great grandchildren—all loved the father who always had time for them. His marriage to Ann Ritchie, a childhood friend—who was also in the WRAF in the First War—was a long and happy one.

Harry Graham lived through the length of the 20th century, in war and peace, in medicine as well as in the service of his country.

He packed an incredible amount of high quality work into that life
time. He had his share of triumph and his full share of difficult
colleagues. His motto was that of the Graham family, whose tartan
he wore so proudly—especially in 1980 when he was elected
Chieftain of the Crieff Highland Games—Ne Oublie—never forget.
But he could also share the motto of the Greenes of County
Kildare in Southern Ireland—nec timeo nec sperno—I neither fear
nor condemn.

William MacIntyre Wilson

William MacIntyre Wilson

JP, MB(Edin), FRCPEd., 10 June 1912–10 June 1975

Bill Wilson's grandfather was a colliery clerk in one of the pits in central Ayrshire in the 19th century. How often was the Wilson family story told and told again in the Scotland of those years. His grandmother was a tiny lady with an indomitable determination that none of her sons would 'go doon the pit' for a living if she could prevent it. Blessed with nimble fingers and clever hands, she saved enough to buy one of Singers' still new-fangled sewing machines. She set up in business sewing for the people of the village, and so successful was she that she earned enough to buy three more machines. Father and sons built an extension at the back of their house, and now mother ran a sewing factory which employed four girls on a permanent basis.

With the income she succeeded in putting all but one of her sons through university. Her eldest, William, after whom Bill was named, became a civil engineer, rose to the rank of Major in the Royal Engineers in the first World War, and later made a fortune in Canada. Three became Church of Scotland Ministers and two Doctors of Medicine, while her only daughter went to the new College of Domestic Science at Atholl Crescent in Edinburgh, took her Diplomas, and married another doctor.

Our Bill's father, John Wilson, was one of the ministers. A handsome man, he was assistant minister at Cardonell in Glasgow when Bill, the eldest of three children, was born. Jessica Jane

Craig, the beautiful daughter of a wealthy industrialist in Ayrshire, had fallen in love with the young man and they were married soon after his ordination. She brought to the family her elegance, and her real talent as a painter. Soon after Bill's birth the family were moved to Perth, where Rev John Wilson was appointed to the charge of St Paul's Church. The manse was in Charlotte Street, but when sister Margaret was born, they moved to a bigger house in the Dundee road. John Wilson went about his duties on a motor bicycle, and in an accident suffered the severest of injuries including a compound fracture of his femur. Because of this, he was not accepted for service when war came.

The next family move was to the parish of Troqueer, in Dumfries, and here the Wilsons lived from 1915 to 1951. The house was a typical Scots manse—old, large, cold, with a huge garden. It was in this home that Bill grew up. His time at Dumfries Academy ended with the Dux medal, and 'so many prizes of books that they had to get the car to carry them all home'.

He went to study medicine in Edinburgh, the ambition of so many Scottish pupils, where the Faculty was world-famous. The traditional story of the Scottish boy of character and cleverness ran true—he educated himself throughout his undergraduate years by the money his bursaries gave him, and had to ask little or nothing from his parents in financial help.

Edinburgh was exciting. He loved his years there. With others, he worked long and hard, going into the wards of the great Royal Infirmary in the evenings to 'clerk'—examine and write case notes for in-patients. This was the recognised way of getting known by the Chief you wanted to work for when you graduated. But there were always more applicants than places, and only the best in the year got the plum posts as 'housemen'.

During the summer vacation of 1934, the Wilson family went to Weem in Perthshire. Fishing was the recreation of the father and his sons, and a permit was bought from the owner of the local hotel. The owner Mr Gordon, who also owned a local farm including three miles of the Tay which he let for fishing, had a daughter called Rhoda. She was training to be a nurse in Edinburgh. She arrived on holiday at the same time as the Wilson family, and in their week together they fell in love. They walked, played tennis, fished together, and talked. Bill had won as a school prize a book of stories about India by Rudyard Kipling, and these tales had fired his enthusiasm to go to India after he qualified and work in the Indian Medical Service. 'He was quite unlike anyone I had ever met', said Rhoda many years later, 'and I knew I wanted to be with him for the rest of my life'.

In the meantime, Bill duly passed his Final Examinations in Edinburgh with distinction. He was chosen by Professor Derrick Dunlop, the recently appointed Professor of Therapeutics, as his first house physician. Then began a friendship which never altered until Bill's death. The young man's aim was to be a physician, and his first and biggest hurdle was the examination for Membership of the Royal College of Physicians of Edinburgh. No training schemes, no registrar posts, no post-graduate facilities were available in those days. So he joined the practice of one of his doctor uncles, Tom Wilson, in the Potteries. He found general practice there exhilirating and challenging. Here was medicine at 'the raw end of pain and poverty'. The great Depression of the '30s was not yet over in that part of Industrial England. He worked hard by night and day. Then, suddenly, he became gravely ill, with the diagnosis of a 'lung abscess'. This was a serious matter in the years when tuberculosis was still rampant and a killer of the young. He was admitted to a TB hospital nearby, and at the end of nine months he was discharged 'cured'.

At once he sat the membership examination for the Royal College and he passed. This was in October 1937. He cabled Rhoda in South Africa, where she was nursing, with the other great news that he had been accepted for the Service, and asked her to come back so that they could be married before Christmas.

27

Their wedding was after Christmas, on 29 December, on a cold dull day. They arrived in Bombay to the heat of India, on 3 April 1938. On their ship were about twenty new appointees to the Indian Medical Service. The voyage with the P and O liner was wonderful. It was a time of total freedom from worry, of good company and food, and exciting ports of call. The excitement of arrival in India was that of so many British—that charm was as great in 1938 as it had been in 1738. India retains a particular, unique drawing power and fascination for British today, but in the late '30s the huge power of the Raj was still dominant. The Wilson's first posting was a lucky one—to Abbotabad on the North West Frontier Province, the 6th Ghurka Training Centre and Headquarters.

In 1938 there was great turmoil in many parts of India. Mahatma Ghandi was the risen political star. His campaign was such that its justice immediately struck fair-minded people like the Wilsons, and it saddened them to realise that there would be many battles, and much suffering before the solution was finally reached. They realised well the crucial geographical and political position of India within the Empire. Their background of hard work and personal endeavour in Scotland made them find the life of the sahib and memsahib somewhat mystifying—the range of personal servants—the boy, syce, dhobie, dirzee, malee—as well as the military ones—was new to them. In 1938, too, came the Munich meeting of Hitler and Mr Neville Chamberlain. Bill had been up much of the previous night stitching many wounds suffered by a young Ghurka who had fallen foul of an irate husband, also having a khukri on issue from the Raj. He was asleep in his chair in the bungalow when the radio announced that it was to be 'peace in our time'.

But there were not to be many afternoon naps for either of them in the next years. Sheila, their first child, was born in February of 1939. Rhoda's father died in Weem four weeks later. Bill was posted with his battalion to a vicious little war on the Afghan

28

border. The Wazirs then as now took pleasure in accurate sniping at the enemy's camps.

The next posting was another border post, Dhera Ismail Khan—but this one safe for families. So they looked for a spell together again. But it was here that Bill Wilson met with an accident as serious as his lung infection of six years before. He ran into an overloaded car—typical of India—which appeared unannounced from one side-road, and was thrown off his army motor cycle into a culvert. He suffered fractured ribs, pelvis and arm, and badly lacerated thigh muscles. He took many months to recover, but after training to get fit again he was posted to Sialkot in the Punjab, tasked with setting up a Training Centre for Field Ambulances. After eight months he was given a special secret posting—for his worth as an officer was now being recognized—to the Middle East, to North Africa. Here he was to visit all the field medical units of the Indian Army serving there and make notes of their problems, to take back to his G.O.C. in India.

The war-time army was by now a meritocracy. After a spell in the Training Centre, he was promoted acting full colonel and ADMS (Assistant Director of Medical Services) of the 9th Indian Armoured Division soon to go to Burma. This was in the summer of 1943. They had a rough time with weather, Mepacrin—a recently issued drug to prevent malaria, and of course the 'Nips'. Casualties were heavy. A number of Indian soldiers taken prisoner elected to fight for the Japanese, and although numbers remained small the problem was a worrying one for military and political staff. So the Indian Army was withdrawn to the border. By contrast, the 10th and 11th Indian Divisions, which had gone to northern Malaya before the war in the Far East began, fought well on their way down the peninsula to eventual enslavement in Singapore.

Next posting was to Paiforce in the Middle East as an ADMS. 'Paiforce' was the force guarding the oil in Persia and Iraq on which the British war effort depended. He remained here till the

29

end of the war in Europe in June of 1945. The family—now three daughters—were at the top of the list for leave in the U.K. home base. Rhoda left India in July 1945 with the children and had an exciting meet with Colonel Wilson at Port Said. Because of security considerations, neither knew the other's movements; they saw each other by pure chance, on the quay. For once the authorities were kindly; they agreed the family could continue home together. Soon after the ship set sail for Britain on 6 August. They heard that the first atomic bomb had been dropped on Hiroshima at 8.15 a.m. Mrs Wilson recalled years later her mixture of fear, awe, and relief as she heard the radio announcement, while she was carrying a tray of baby food from the dining saloon of the ship. Relief was the main emotion. All soldiers knew that a war of attrition against the Japanese would mean a million dead on the allied side alone. And all our own Japanese P.O.W. would be murdered—they had had to dig their own graves shortly before the first bomb fell. But there was now a future to look forward to once again, a brief spell back with parents at Dumfries, and to Rhoda's mother and relatives in Abernyte near Dundee.

In the spring of 1946 he received his next and final posting as an officer of the British Empire in India. Its full title was 'Surgeon to His Excellency the Commander-in-Chief' (Field Marshall Sir Claud Auchinleck). Colonel Wilson regarded this plum posting—for such it was—with trepidation. Not only was he 'The Auk's' personal physician, but he was to command the Army Medical Service at HQ New Delhi. The whole headquarters included in all some 2,000–3,000 officers, men and families. He had overall responsibility for the 'Lady Willingdon' Hospital, and he ran a clinic every morning for senior officers and their wives.

The Victory Parade in London was on 6 June 1946. The Commander-in-Chief India flew in his own plane to lead the Indian contingent. Before he left, he called in his personal physician. 'Would you like me to bring your wife back with me, Bill?' A signal to Rhoda to be prepared to leave with her children for India in a week's time was sent: classification—immediate. This was the level at which Bill Wilson was now working.

All serving British officers were now being offered terms of redundancy, as summer progressed. Lord Mountbatten replaced Lord Wavell as Viceroy. His remit from the Attlee government was: 'Independence by 15 August—come what may'.

During this anxious summer, Field Marshal Auchinleck came regularly into the Wilson home to talk, play with the children, and relax from his daily strains and anxieties. In public Auchinleck was the 'servant of Government' but in this home he could talk freely of his fears and his anger—for he knew Bill Wilson was a doctor, and a man trained from childhood to keep a confidence totally. Sometimes 'the Chief' would invite the Wilson children to his garden to play—to try to catch his goldfish from their pond, and play with him and the children of his gardener.

The Field Marshall advised Bill to send his family away, so great did the danger become that summer. And then Colonel Wilson and the others in the Indian Army of Great Britain did what the politicians wanted—they left India. It took the assassination of Gandhi to stun the nation out of its insensate killing. Independence arrived. Perhaps one day it would be remembered that many British did work hard to help that Independence arrive. Perhaps by next century the real friendship that existed between all races in the Indian Army would be re-discovered by the historian. And Bill Wilson and Rhoda walked through History in that summer. At a party in government House Pandit Nehru was talking with Bill—not *to* him, but *with* him. Smiling, he said 'We could do with men like you. Stay with us'.

Back in Edinburgh, Colonel Wilson became Dr W. M. Wilson, unpaid Clinical Tutor to Sir Derrick Dunlop. The family settled down into a house much smaller and very much less servanted than the Residence of the C in C's Personal Physician in New Delhi! In 1949 he was appointed Consultant Physician at the Royal Infirmary in Perth, with his senior colleague Dr Ian Easton.

31

Ian Easton was an outstanding physician with a good war record also. Brilliant, unreliable, given to disappearances but the soul of kindness on his return, Dr Easton could have held a Chair of Medicine. While Bill's humour was that of the quiet smile, Ian's was that of the hearty laugh. On his way overseas to his own war, Major Easton went into an operating theatre in Gibraltar. He was bemused at the surgeon passing his cystoscope into the urethras and bladders of a succession of soldiers and withdrawing the instrument dripping with blood. The Dundee theatre orderly was unimpressed. 'The Major aye draws blood wi' his telescope' he confided to the newly arrived physician.

Together they would become the best team of physicians in Tayside. They were both exceedingly good in complementary ways—the solidity of care and extensive knowledge of Dr Wilson complemented the extensive knowledge and intuitive diagnostic skill of Dr Easton. The flair for endocrine disease—especially for the treatment of diabetes and thyroid diseases—of Dr Wilson complemented the flair for heart and chest disease of Dr Easton. Dr Wilson covered the sometime absences of Dr Easton without a murmur—though his wife complained occasionally. Not only did they treat adults, they treated children, and their joint opinion was better than that of any of the paediatricians contemporary to them. So they covered the widest range of medicine possible for their times—the twenty years from 1949 till 1969—and this was what gave them the extra no others reached.

Perth was now their settled home. A house in the country—Rockdale (later signposted 'Dr Wilson's house')—and the prospect of being able to put down roots—literally, as they planted trees on their twenty acres of land—made this longest portion of their lives happy. Their second son, John, now Providentially and happily placed in kindly Kirkcaldy another physician of the Wilson family—was born there. There were many problems—the division between the Royal Infirmary, the establishment hospital, and the bigger wartime Emergency Medical Service hutted hospital at Bridge of

Earn—being the main one. As always, the newly arrived staff in the latter felt themselves better than the older, apparently less active, staff in the older organisation. As always, the older established staff could not really see what all the fuss was about.

During these twenty years, Dr Bill Wilson always knew patients as people. The Thatcher mentality of describing them as 'clients' would have abhorred his deepest instincts. He brought up his family to accept that patients must at all times come first if they needed his help. He had a wonderfully dry sense of humour—of a particularly Scottish sort. His expression, or his twitch of a cheek muscle, could make someone laugh. A photograph of him shows his one stern eye (his left) and his other laughing eye (his right). He loved fishing, and taught his five children to fish. Perhaps his garden was an even greater love, but he somehow never had enough time to spend in it. To patients who had to be given bad news he sometimes said 'But remember God has the last word'.

Perhaps he was lucky to do the largest slice of his life's work in the early years of the National Health Service, before the Keith Joseph reforms began its decline and fall and in due course patient care was replaced by patient cost. He had wished to serve his fellow women and men in India; now in a Health Service available free to all he could do so in Scotland. He did no private practice. These first twenty five years were the happy ones—adequate funds, involvement of local people in running the service, and doctors and nurses working hard because they wanted to, not because there was a manager at their back urging yet more and more productivity out of them, like a 19th century foreman with his stick.

He was unique amongst Perth physicians in establishing himself a position of authority on the Dundee medical scene. His especial skill in managing diabetes led to his doing a weekly diabetic clinic at the invitation of Professor Sir Ian Hill for problem cases, with Dr Robert Semple. This was on a Wednesday. Because he was so modest, the very existence of this clinic was unknown to many of his fellows.

33

Though such a kind and loving man, Bill Wilson was no sentimentalist. He stood out against the malice of doctor against doctor so prevalent in the Perth of his day. When he saw dishonesty, he challenged it at once. A famous actor wrote a sneering, damaging letter to the *Scotsman* about a man Bill Wilson had known well. 'Mr ... is a liar and a coward'. Bill wrote next day. 'A liar, because what he says is untrue. A coward, because the man is dead and will not answer back'. He saw a younger colleague about to be victimised, he was certain, by more than one member of staff. The colleague was called into the medical superintendent's office. Bill Wilson came in too, determined to see fair play. The individual was in fact victimised after Bill's death, and his remaining years were lonely and unhappy. For him, the death of Bill Wilson was the most important event of his medical life.

In June of 1975, Ted, husband of his daugher Libby, had arranged a fishing holiday for him in the Galloway hills he loved so much. From their base at Gatehouse of Fleet they drove and then climbed up a hill to the loch on the morning of the 10th—his birthday, both trying to ignore the fact that each was a little breathless—Ted went ahead to untie the boat—he heard Bill say 'Isn't this just perfect?' Then he heard a thud—Bill had fallen, struck his head against a wooden stake, and fallen into about a foot of water at the loch's edge. Ted quickly pulled him out, but he was dead from a heart attack. He was 63 years old.

Bill Wilson's untimely death was not only a devastating shock to his friends and to the patients who loved him so much. It was a watershed in the history of Perth medicine, coming as it did at the beginning of the reductions in services now being proposed by recently designated 'management'. Also, hospital amalgamations meant that long-standing resentments could easily burst into flames. He, and he alone—for there was no-one after his death with the independent strength of character, the selfless integrity, and above all the ability to see both sides—who could have spoken

34

kindly to the contestants and resolved their differences. Seldom in the story of a small medical community could the loss of one person be so important.

At his funeral service, St John's Kirk was packed. 'Today we remember dear Bill Wilson' said Alan Young, its minister. Dr Ronald McNeill, his younger colleague, later to become the next senior physician in Perthshire, helped to carry his coffin on his shoulders. Most hospital staff—but not all—were present. Many doctors were there. 'Did you know Dr Wilson?' Rev Uist Macdonald asked a woman leaving the church. She replied simply 'He saved my life'. Several of us wept unashamedly. We knew how much we had lost. But we knew the trumpets sounded for Bill on the other side.

William Lofley Tullis

Dr William Lofley Tullis

MD(St Andrews), DPH, 1896–1975

Below Perth the Tay receives the Earn with the Farg and becomes a full sized river. Our next doctor first saw Newburgh, on the Fife side, when he was a schoolboy, and towards the end of his life he recalled 'when I saw Lindores Loch I thought it was the loveliest spot I had ever seen—the spring sunshine on the water. When I reached the village I had to get off my bicycle because the streets were cobbled ... There were trees lining the roadway, and houses with outside stairs—some of them with thatched roofs'.

William Tullis was born in Newport in 1896. His father was a master tailor in Dundee, and had his shop in Reform Street. His mother's father was a sea-captain from Hull—when he was first mate on the good ship *Diana*, he was stuck in the polar ice in Franz Joseph Land for six months. Later, as captain of his own ships, he was an explorer and whaler. He was captain William Lofley, and it was from his grandfather that our William Tullis got his middle name.

He went first to the junior school in Newport and next to The High School of Dundee. There he was outstanding in rugby and athletics, and was Dux of the School in 1914. Prizes and a bursary took him to St Andrews University to study medicine, but in 1916 he volunteered to join the Royal Navy and was soon commissioned as a surgeon sublieutenant probationary.

He had what can only be described as a very eventful war;

seeing service in Gallipoli, the Mediterranean with the 10th Naval Flotilla, on the Dover Patrol, and covering the landings at Zeebrugge and Heligoland. While in the Mediterranean he met by chance his 8 years older brother who was serving as an engineering officer on another ship. His brother graduated as an engineer at St Andrews after the war and became a Professor of Engineering at Patna in India.

William's ships were the *St Margaret of Scotland*, then HMS *Princess Ena*, and finally the cruiser HMS *Europa*. He carried out appendicectomies on each of these, though only a first year medical student! Twice he was mentioned in despatches.

Back to St Andrews once the war was over he went, but sadly without many of his contemporaries. 'I lost three-quarters of my class-mates'. He graduated MB in 1922, and was Professor Price's houseman in DRI. At this stage public health interested him. So he took the DPH in 1924, and moved to the north of England. First he was resident surgical officer at the Blackburn and East Lancashire Hospital, then he became deputy medical officer of health at Middlesbrough. Soon he became MOH for the River Tees, and consultant to the fever and smallpox hospital at Hemlington. Here he contributed to the medical journals and wrote a thesis for the MD of St Andrews. The thesis was accepted in 1926 and awarded distinction—'Smallpox in Middlesbrough 1875–1925 with Original Observations on the Present Epidemic'. In Middlesbrough he met Inga, his wife, at the Scottish Presbyterian Church in Linthorpe Road, where they both worshipped. The church continues as a meeting place for the many Scots who work in the Middlesbrough area.

But William Tullis had never forgotten Tayside. The Tees was no substitute for the glorious Tay. In 1928 he heard that a practice was becoming available in Newburgh. He asked Professor Price's advice: 'Do you think I should think about it?' 'Tullis, take it' replied Professor Price. 'It's a very good one.'

And so on a cold snowy day in February 1928 he arrived in the

Fife town which he was to serve with total dedication for 43 years. To Ivybank, the Georgian house in the High Street which was the practice premises he arrived with his new wife—they were married in 1929. The house had been the surgery for two distinguished predecessors—Dr Gunn and Dr Niven. There were still the stables where Dr Niven kept his pony and trap, and there was still the speaking tube for night callers between the outside street and the doctor's bedroom. In the town, an influenza epidemic was raging.

And now began a life-time of devotion to everyone and everything almost unsurpassable in its quality. Newburgh was at that time still a town with industry—the linoleum factory—and was flourishing. Lindores Abbey was nearby, and the monks as always picked their site wisely. Fruit trees flourished, the port was busy in earlier centuries and there was a linen factory. Still there was pottery making, farming, and salmon fishing. Sheep were taken over by boat to Mugdrum Island. Electricity was only just coming into people's homes.

The practice extended far for one doctor and his assistant. To the Perth side it went as far as Aberargie—beyond Abernethy. From there it marched south by Glenfoot, east over the hills to Pitcairlie farm on the Auchtermuchty road, and then north to Birkhill, Luthrie, and back 'all by the river'. In those years there were many more farms, all with many more workers, than there are today.

Ivybank provided a 24 hour service. There were no appointments. Dr Tullis would always answer a call at once—he would rise from his meal and never wait till he had finished. Although surgery times were 9–10 a.m. and 6–7 p.m., the evening surgery often continued till 10 p.m. 'Patients came and went all day', Mrs Tullis remembered. 'Because the farms were so scattered, it was a job finding him sometimes, but 'phones when they arrived were a great help in tracking him down. We gave up the speaking tube!'

As well as help as receptionist, hold down patients who were having teeth extracted (for Dr Tullis was the local dentist too), and strive to locate the doctor on his rounds, she did the books. 'It was 1/6 (7½ pence) a visit, later 2/- (10 pence). Confinements were 2 guineas but rose to £3. We had 2,000 patients in the Abernethy part of the practice and 4,000 in the Newburgh part—but they were very scattered.'

Some paid in kind, rather than cash. Many of the poorer patients did not pay, especially when only the husband was 'on the panel'.

A half day or so a week was possible, as there was always an assistant. These remained a year and covered the whole spectrum of doctor from excellent to drunken but kindly. Surgery included stitching of wounds, removal of small lumps, and of foreign bodies from fish hooks to impaled tree trunks. Ears were pierced and some animals treated. Dr Tullis' three children—they had two daughters and a son—as they grew older were allowed to hold the magnifying glass while fine surgery was being done. Holiday was two weeks a year—not more 'except 17 days once when we went for a cruise'. 'But we were comfortably off.'

Every sort of incident occurred over the years. Drunken men, young women in distress, prisoners in custody, tinkers advanced in abnormal labour (four confinements in one night was by no means unusual—sometimes the howdie* had got into trouble, which meant both doctors working), injured workers from the factory, the quarry, the fishing boats or the farms, children drowned in the Tay, were all in a year's work. Patients needing admission to Perth Royal Infirmary were taken by Mrs Tullis in the doctor's car, until Dr Tullis managed to obtain an ambulance—then kept in his old stables. He went by boat to Mugdrum Island, and in bad winters—especially 1947, around the farms on horseback.

For Dr Tullis was an expert horseman. He owned a tall horse of 17 hands which he kept at Denmuir Farm and rode two or three times a week. Sometimes he rode with the Fife hunt, but he was

*unqualified midwife.

not a hunting enthusiast. His other sport was shooting—not of game but he preferred target and clay pigeon. This he could do both at the TA drill hall range at Newburgh or at the club at Higham. He was an excellent shot.

So the years went on. Dr Tullis started *everything* in Newburgh and Abernethy—the British Legion, the junior football club, the bowling club, the Earl Haig fund, the Old Peoples' Welfare association. He enjoyed curling on his beloved Lindores Loch. He lectured in first-aid to the railwaymen of Newburgh and Perth, and examined in first-aid throughout Scotland. He was the unofficial but deeply trusted marriage counsellor, and the legal adviser to many of his people. 'Everyone went to the doctor.' The Newburgh market was the great affair of the year, held every June. New dresses were bought in Perth specially for it. Illnesses were reckoned as having started 'before' or 'after' the market. Salmon continued to fall accidentally off fish lorries and be gifted to the doctor. Patients still came and went all day long, certain of a patient and sympathetic hearing. In 1939 came the Second War, and one bomb fell near Newburgh—a jettison from a Junkers returning from the big raid on Clydebank. Dr Tullis became Captain Tullis, RMO of the 1st Fife Bn. of the Home Guard. In 1947 ex-Queen Ena of Spain was the guest of the Duchess of Westminster at Moncreiffe House, she took ill, and a Dundee surgeon recommended Dr W. L. Tullis to attend her. He had served on a ship bearing her name 30 years before.

Dr Tullis was in no way limited or solitary in his professional life and contacts. As well as his succession of assistants, he had colleagues in Fife whom he knew well. Those from Cupar, Auchtermuchty, Wormit and Newport, formed a medical club which not only met socially in one another's houses, but conducted medical audit of the times and discussed illness and practice problems.

Dr Hugh Muir of Auchtermuchty, a famous Fife doctor who was in his turn Chairman of the Scottish Council of the BMA,

41

wrote a wonderful 'This is your life' address to Dr Tullis on his retiral, and it was supported by many Fife medical friends.

In 1948 came the National Health Service. Now free medical care was available to all. Like his contemporaries, Dr Tullis welcomed and blessed this change. Though part of his devoted life was regular visiting of patients—especially the older ones—even if they did not make a call, but 'just to pop in to see how they were'—he knew that the embarrassment of feeling they had to pay was now lifted from his dear old friends.

The NHS came 20 years after he began his practice in Newburgh and Abernethy. Hospital practice became wider in its extent also, and another huge benefit was the uniform salary scales country wide for hospital staff. No more were the peripheral areas short of specialists of as high calibre as the larger, richer cities. This would prevail until threatened by the ill-considered government plans of the later 1980s. Dr Tullis was a respected colleague of Drs Easton and Wilson, of Mr Conal Charleson and Mr Roger Kirkpatrick, Miss Elliot and Mr Ian Fraser, all of the nearby Royal Infirmary. He respected them all greatly, and also respected the staff of the new and large Bridge of Earn Hospital—Mr Smillie and his many colleagues, and our friend Harry Graham.

In 1966 a new young surgeon was appointed. Dr Tullis heard he was a St Andrews graduate—a rarity in either nearby hospital. He telephoned him, introduced himself as a fellow alumnus, and in the nicest possible way indicated to him that he would refer patients to him, and if he turned out reliable, would refer all his patients for surgical treatment! He must have found the young man satisfactory, as not only did he refer practice patients, but his own family—including his grandson—to the young man.

In 1967 he had been nearly 40 years the doctor of Newburgh. So dearly was he loved, and so hugely was he respected, that the town made him a Freeman of the Burgh. He was only the second Freeman in 500 years.

'The Provost, Magistrates and Councillors of the Burgh of Newburgh in Fife at a meeting held on 11th January 1967 unanimously agreed to confer the Freedom of the Burgh on WILLIAM LOFLEY TULLIS MD, DPH TO HONOUR HIM FOR HIS LONG AND DEVOTED SERVICE TO THE COMMUNITY' read the scroll.

The Provost was Mr Angus Goodall. A tape recording of the ceremony remains to give a quality of remembrance no written word can convey—the sincerity of the councillors, the warmth of the applause, the happiness and deserved pride in Dr Tullis' reply. And in 1970, the Burgh of Abernethy made him a Freeman of theirs—Provost Morrison said it all again. Seldom can a doctor anywhere have had such universal love and respect, gratitude and admiration. But seldom unless perhaps in a prison camp, can one man have doctored to an entire population and given his life to them.

The other event of 1970 was the opening of the new clinic in Newburgh. This marked the end of one era—the doctor's home being the surgery and open to all—and the beginning of another—the appointments system, the team care, the ample off-duty for the new generation of family practitioners. To the new clinic Dr Tullis presented his desk.

In 1971 he retired. A third time a recording was made for posterity. The old public hall was packed. The gift was commensurate with the people's gratitude and affection—and also with their generosity. The retiral presentation followed a concert in the Tayside Institute. Dr Tullis again spoke quietly, humorously, kindly. He was a good story teller. You can almost see the kindness of his face as you listen to him speak.

Of course he continued to drop in on his former patients—now as a friend, no longer as their doctor. How sad that the habit of the regular dropping in on patients has gone—at least by a majority of doctors. One hospital specialist saw a patient at his follow-up clinic who complained mildly that his practitioner had not visited him since his return home a month before. When he mentioned this in his letter to the practice, he received an immediate reply telling him 'It is not our practice to visit patients discharged from hospitals unless in very special circumstances!'

Dr Tullis and Dr Wilson were great friends, and shared the same ideals of service. Bill's sudden death saddened him greatly. His own death was also a rather sudden one. He had consulted Dr Wilson about his angina for a number of years and now missed his counsel. One evening, after he had dropped in on an old friend in her home, he felt unwell. Admitted to the Royal Infirmary, he remained comfortable over the next day, but died in the evening. This was 7 July 1975.

Seldom can a doctor have been so universally admired. The only criticism ever made of him was that he might have retired earlier—but he loved his work too much to do this. He is another famous man to be praised.

Martin Fallon

Martin Fallon

OBE, MCh, FRCSI, FRCS

Our next medical man is a link between the City of Dundee and the City of Perth for he practised in both. He was born in 1909 at Newcastle West, near Limerick. His father, a constable in the Royal Irish Constabulary, was born in Sligo, his mother, Catherine O'Brien, in Kerry. It was a rule of the R.I.C. that you could not serve in the county of your own or your wife's birth, so Kevin Fallon was posted to Limerick in 1907.

In 1916 when Martin was seven years old, the Irish revolution began. His schoolmaster refused to correct his school work, and the other children attacked him, because his father was in the R.I.C. His school days were unhappy and lonely. Things became so bad that in 1920 the family left their home—virtually as refugees—and settled in Chester. His father's pension was advanced—to 17 years from seven, but he had to bring up a wife and eight children on £4 5s 0d a month. 'My mother saved for our education' Martin recalled in his old age. 'She was a wonderful woman'. He pointed to her photograph on his table. 'My father gave up and lost interest in everything when he had to leave Ireland. Mother went back to Dublin in 1925 for the funeral of an aunt. When she got back to Chester, she said "the shooting's over"—so we went back'.

Martin was one of several of the clever members of his family. Money was saved; he went to Trinity to study Medicine and graduated in 1932. Here his years were happier; he made friends,

47

enjoyed himself, and put his earlier sadness behind him. What did he do for house jobs? 'I looked up the BMJ. I saw a house surgeon's post in Huddersfield, and I started there three days later'.

His year at Trinity was a smaller one than usual. Before 1927, graduates went automatically on the British Registrar but that year 'The Republicans wanted nothing to do with Britain. So they started an Irish register. All that happened was that many Irish doctors practising in England immediately sent their sons to Oxford or Cambridge—not Trinity. So our year had only about 60 members compared with the usual 80'.

Martin enjoyed the North of England. After Huddersfield he moved to Hope Hospital, Salford, and he remained in that area for five years from graduation. He took his Fellowship, and later MCh of Trinity by examination—a difficult hurdle. But there was no thesis. His special subject was urinary surgery, then as now an interest in Salford.

In 1937 his dear mother died of a breast cancer. His father outlived her for ten years. Martin had always been poor in financial terms—England had paid better than Dublin—but he felt he should return, to stay near his father. He was appointed assistant surgeon at Sir Patrick Dun's Hospital in Dublin, and Tutor in Anatomy at Trinity, 'I was lucky', he recalled—'You must remember the Roman Catholic majority made it very difficult for Protestants to get in—St Vincent's and the Mater, for example, were for Catholics only'. This fact, regularly forgotten when the North of Ireland is accused of bigotry, militated against someone like Martin—with his background of Royal Irish Constabulary and his acceptance of Protestantism though baptised by a priest, and he did well to gain the post he did. Now he was in surgery and anatomy—two subjects he liked and was good at. Still he was poor—his salary £200 *per annum*, increased by as much tutoring and cramming in anatomy as he could find time for.

With the outbreak of the Second World War began the formative years of his life as a man and as a surgeon. But once

48

again he had a set-back which upset him very much. 'There were about ten of us from Dublin who wanted to go the War—not the most popular wish as far as many of the Dubliners were concerned—I went to Belfast on the 4th of September—the day after the outbreak'. (His younger brother Ted had graduated in the summer of 1939 and gone to the RAMC at once—no requirement for pre-registration house posts then. 'He had a hard war, developed cerebral malaria in Burma, and became mentally ill—later progressing to suicide—after he returned in 1945'.) When he was medically examined at the Grand Central Hotel the doctor said 'You are diabetic. Your urine is full of sugar'. 'Try testing it yourself', he offered, seeing Martin's amazement and anger.

Back he went to Dublin, puzzled and discomfited. After a series of tests he was found to have sugar in his urine as a result of an inborn abnormality of his kidneys. 'It took me six months', he recalled later. 'But by March 1940, armed with my papers and reports, I went back to Belfast'. This time he was accepted, and soon found himself at Beckett's Park at Leeds, 'where all the Scots and (Northern) Irish went to do their basic RAMC training'.

'I found myself on a train bound for Dover that June—when we arrived, we found 350,000 men coming the other way. I remember one who shouted at us "Jesus Christ—get back the other way". So our train shunted, and back we all went. We were meeting the survivors of the defeat in France.'

Next he found himself in the Middle East, first in Syria and Palestine, then in Alexandria. There he worked in the surgical division with Majors J. C. Watts and P. Thompson from Dingwall. Here occurred an incident of interest. St Mary's House on the west side of Alexandria was a favourite club for officers. One night, it suffered a direct hit by a bomb, and Martin worked through the night, treating and operating on both visitors and staff. 'I was put up for a DSO by the Royal Navy' he recalled later—'as there were so many naval officers present—some quite senior. But it was not proceeded with because, d'ye see, St Mary's was an officers' brothel.'

Promoted Lieutenant-Colonel he returned to UK by way of Malta and Naples. Like all his contemporaries, he had put in a vast amount of operating time and seen a life-time of surgery in a very few years. Now he would grow into more senior rank and higher responsibility, with the Allied Forces of the Invasion of Europe. He was specially selected and promoted quickly, such was his reputation as a fearless, tireless surgeon. A set-back in Malta was an illness from a duodenal ulcer, but he recovered quickly.

So much happened from D Day onwards. Two events out of a multitude we will record—the first his contribution to the Arnhem battle. He was O.C. surgical division in 39 General Hospital, placed in a Brussels hospital ('a huge place, with acres of grounds') immediately after the liberation. 'After we had all been kissed on both cheeks, we got on with Montgomery's plan to win the war all on his own'.

His account of the Arnhem battle is a fascinating one, and his own contribution told almost dismissively. Two hospitals took casualties on alternate days; his took 5825 casualties in 13 days. 'So did my opposite number in the nearby General Hospital,' he recalled. 'So we were both busy. We both got the OBE'. 'Most of the casualties were from the forces trying to link up with the paras—I remember the Irish Guards were the lead regiment in the Guards Armoured Division. They were told by Monty to drive along the main road two-a-breast, as it was so wide. The German 88s knocked them off the road like ninepins—two at a time'.

The second was his most famous patient of the War—William Joyce—Lord Haw-Haw.

On the evening of 28 May 1945, Joyce was walking through a wood which overlooked the harbour at Flensburg. He saw two British officers gathering wood and for some unbelievable reason called out helpfully in English 'there are a few more pieces over here' and was recognized by one of them, Lieutenant Perry. Perry, thinking Joyce was going to draw a revolver, shot him first. The bullet fired at close range passed through Joyce's right thigh, through his perineum, and out of his left thigh. Taken prisoner, Joyce was brought by ambulance to 71 General Hospital at Flensburg Heath, beside the British Second Army Headquarters. The O.C. surgical division was Lieutenant-Colonel Martin Fallon.

'Joyce had five holes in his arse when he was brought in to me' recalled Martin with his usual style of wit. 'When he left he had had four extra ones closed'. He was put under severe pressure from the military police to hand Joyce over at once, but he refused. Pressurised again, he sought and obtained help from his DDMS, Brigadier Glyn Hughes, to have the patient kept in his care until his wounds were healed. Then, and only then, did Colonel Fallon agree to his removal. Things became quieter thereafter. Martin formed a friendship with Lieutenant-Colonel R. J. Kellar, his opposite in the surgical division of 73 General Hospital at Hamburg; Kellar would in later years become Professor of Obstetrics at Edinburgh University.

The War over, he found himself back in Dublin, as assistant surgeon at Sir Patrick Dun's hospital: 'Dublin was full of small hospitals'. But he was also still a university demonstrator in anatomy at Trinity, besides being on the surgical staff. Martin Fallon had in mind to go into anatomy. He thought of moving to Cambridge, where he knew Professor C. P. Wilson, with the aim of applying in the course of time for the Chair at Trinity. He had a flair for this subject—he could draw and teach with clarity and great skill. His former students remembered his ability to make this so-difficult-to-teach subject fascinating to them. But he chose surgery. He was by now 39 years old. Forty years later, Martin Fallon acknowledged his mistake. Though he was unaware of it in 1947, this was a crisis in his life. He could—and probably should—have become an anatomist. He could very well have been appointed to a Chair, which he would have embellished, and become a legend in his own life time with a generation or more of students. 'But I was so taken up with surgery' he confessed, a little sadly. 'I had had a good war and I saw myself going onwards and

51

C

upwards. I would also perhaps have been better if I'd stayed in the Army. I was offered a Brigadier's post and a posting to India but turned it down'.

His interest in thoracic surgery had come about before the war. T. B. Nelson, a London thoracic surgeon, had a large collection of chest instruments—trochars and the like, and a group of American surgeons whom Martin met in Paris asked him if he could help them to buy some and take them by ship to the States. They were so short of dollars that they couldn't do this themselves. So he sailed out on the SS *Lucania* with his US friends to Boston, where he watched and learned some chest surgery at the Lahey clinic. For a short time during the war he had met Mr Bruce Dick, thoracic surgeon at Hairmyres Hospital in the west of Scotland, and had gone to visit his wards and assist in the theatre. After the war he made another trip to the U.S.A., and once more interested himself in chest surgery. It was on a visit to Dublin by Mr Bruce Dick that his later career was decided. Dick told him of the post-war plans to establish thoracic surgical centres in Scotland, mainly Glasgow, Edinburgh and Aberdeen but in a smaller way in Dundee. He asked Mr Fallon to apply, oiled the wheels of his application, and he was duly appointed by the Eastern Regional Hospital Board.

Thus it was when he came to Ashludie in 1948 as consultant surgeon to the Eastern Regional Thoracic Surgical Service that his connection with Tayside began. He married Hazel Spink, one of the daughters of that famous family. In 1950, Charles, the first of their three sons, was born in Edinburgh. Lieutenant-Colonel R. J. Kellar, now Professor of Obstetrics at Edinburgh, made good his war-time promise to help when Martin was married and a child came along. In 1952 his second son Michael, who while at St Andrews became one of the bright young Tory thinkers congregated at that university in the early 1970's, and who later became member of parliament for Darlington, personal private secretary to Cecil Parkinson and later a Tory whip, was born.

Nigel, the third son, was born in 1956, in Perth like Michael. Mr Ian Fraser was now their obstetrician. The family home was created out of five cottages on Invergowrie bay, and was decorated by Hazel Fallon with her own taste and elegance. They called it 'Tayside'. Here the boys grew up.

Now he had his own unit; he was his own master. Dr David Smith was the physician superintendent of the chest hospital at Ashludie, and in 1948 'chest hospital' meant 'sanatorium for pulmonary tuberculosis'. This disease was still one of dread— students were taught to call it 'Koch's infection' in the wards, because of the awful connotation of the word 'tuberculosis'. But now the drug Streptomycin had arrived, and chemotherapy of tuberculosis was possible for the first time.

Yet Streptomycin could not cure all patients, especially not those whose lungs were afflicted by chronic disease. Tubercle was the first great enemy Martin Fallon would have to tackle. Operations involved the removal of part of a lung, called lobectomy. But it also involved the large and often bloody operation called thoracoplasty, when a number, often a large number, of ribs were removed, allowing the wall of the chest to collapse on the apex of the lung where tubercle always struck. This compressed the apex of the lung, often with a chronic cavity of phthisis in it, and, along with treatment by Streptomycin, eventually cured the patient.

The other great disease was carcinoma of the lung. In 1948 this was almost a 'new disease' and it would explode into a virtual epidemic of one of the most angry cancers in the western world. Martin Fallon was in on the first act of this dramatic disease and over the next 20 years would battle with it in company with his fellow chest surgeons in Edinburgh, Glasgow and Aberdeen. They would have to learn the technique of bronchoscopy and would have to work with radiologists, radiotherapists and chest physicans. They would have to learn the natural history of the disease and which techniques would succeed and which fail. The natural history of tuberculosis was already well known, but what was not known was how surgery—a totally new branch of surgery—might hasten cure and improve the outlook here too.

Martin Fallon established his reputation not only as a bold surgeon while he was at Ashludie. He established his reputation as a *character*. A succession of registrars on the training rotation came to work in his unit, as well as his senior registrars with whom he generally fought. They learned his mannerisms—his 'D'you follow me?' ... 'Is that quite clear?' He could be irascible—very irascible, and his comments on colleagues or indeed anyone could be pungent and penetrating. But on the other hand his Irish charm, his wit, his great ability to tell an entertaining anecdote, made him a delightful companion also. His isolation from other surgical units in the town, his bow ties, plus his reputation as a talker and critic, made him something of a celebrity. His nursing staff were as loyal and as fond of him as their opposite numbers in the other surgical units were of their chiefs—of that there is no doubt.

Did he do any cardiac surgery? He did no more than excise the pericardium in patients with scarring of that part of the heart; with his fellow thoracic surgeons he had decided, as early as 1951, that no further cardiac units were necessary in Scotland beyond the three then established in Glasgow, Edinburgh and Aberdeen. Professor Kenneth Lowe recalled his kindness to patients referred from the cardiac unit of Sir Ian Hill, and how successful his operative skill was, many years after he left Ashludie.

And then a new Professor, Donald Douglas, was appointed to St Andrews in 1951. He had come from Edinburgh where he was first assistant to the great Sir James Learmonth, Professor of Surgery there. Learmonth's interest was vascular surgery, but Professor Douglas sought to establish a cardiac surgery unit in Dundee. He had had no training in the specialty. The first cardiac surgery in Dundee had already been done by the brilliant technician F. R. Brown, who tied the patent ductus in children. Professor Douglas carried on closed heart surgery for rheumatic heart disease with success, but his unit never had the expertise to go permanently into the open heart field. Martin Fallon was critical of the professorial unit during its early years, since he did not consider there would ever be enough work to justify it or to give its staff experience and safety. There was an element of rivalry; the Professor held trump cards but not all.

Inevitably, his chest unit, since it carried out only surgery of the lungs, began to run down. This was inevitable, as tuberculosis came more and more under control by the newer drugs available, and there were fewer and fewer cases to operate on. Cancer of the lung continued, but many cases were inoperable by the time the patient came to the doctor. In the 1960's, then, discussions were begun between Mr Fallon and the Regional Board about how his diminishing work load might be increased. Eventually, after long discussions, it was agreed that he be moved to Perth, to do general surgery but retain a number of beds for the chest surgery still needed in the region.

His move there was unfortunately not welcomed by many of the local staff. Perth medicine had been divided for 10 years into the establishment hospital, the Royal Infirmary, and the larger Emergency Medical Services Hospital at Bridge of Earn. Sadly, bitter attacks were made by Bridge of Earn staff on those they saw as having all the favours—University appointments, students to teach, private practice, and the pick of the local patients. Some Bridge of Earn staff had as their life ambition to be consultants at Perth Royal and were ambivalent in their attitudes, but the large and important orthopaedic department—with no such ambitions— were the fiercest critics of the older institution.

His feelings on his arrival in October 1967, in succession to Mr Conal Charleson—himself an autocrat who had made life hard for those he saw as incomers—were of some trepidation. He had spent several months in the USA re-learning abdominal surgery, and the other components of 'general surgery' of the day, but his practical experience was lacking. The account by Dr John Millers, his

55

anaesthetist, of how a number of apparently very concerned staff had gone to the Board ostensibly to complain about the handling of patients by his predecessor Mr Charleson—but in fact with the aim of discrediting. and destroying him—did not increase his confidence!

So his seven years at Perth were not happy. Cruel gossip and unfair innuendo was repeated against him. Yet he worked with dignity and courage, and his much younger colleague remembered his seven years with Martin as his 'golden years'. His irascible temper did not endear him to all—his outspoken comment, especially on certain staff—his teasing of nursing staff—could be sharp. 'If that man came to wash our windows', he said of a doctor in an investigative specialty, 'I'd say to Hazel: "watch the silver!"' But his skill in dissecting lung cancer remained, and he carried out a number of very major operations with success.

By now he was in his 60's and tired more easily. Travel for emergency work from Invergowrie was especially fatiguing. As with every surgeon who gets old, he began to become a little less sure, a little less confident. This was especially so with injured accident victims; Sister Geddes recalled 20 years later her sympathy when he trembled visibly, confronted with severe multiple injuries. The confident surgeon who had sorted out the casualties of St Mary's House had now aged as all of us will inevitably do. The severe mental illness of his eldest son, too, shortly before his retiral in 1974, was a cruel blow to one so proud. He told no one, except his younger colleague and Dr Wilson, and both men respected him for ever afterwards for his courage and his efforts to accept perhaps the worst blow of his life.

His remaining years were solitary. Away from his wife, he lived them in Kincarrathie House in Perth. He was forgotten by almost everyone. More and more he lived in the past, recalling his war-time exploits, his years in Ashludie, the great men he had known. 'If I had any belief' he said to a younger friend who visited him too seldom 'I'd have a different attitude to life'.

56

His flashes of wit and perception, and his pride, never left him. He wittily entertained staff at Perth when taken there to have a small wart removed by a plastic surgeon. Sister Halliday, his first ward sister at Perth, felt all her former affection for him flow back when she saw him at the Perth Festival, in a party of elderly from Kincarrathie. 'Look at me amongst all these old women with their blue rinses' he quipped. Professor W. F. Walker, who treated his near-gangrenous feet in Ninewells in 1988, found himself still treated as he had been when he was Martin's registrar—'Is that quite clear, Walker? D'ye follow me, Walker?'

His 80th birthday in February 1989 was an event which re-kindled his pride. 'I read *The Times* ' he told a visitor, 'every day. I've noticed how many depart in their 70's. Only the best of us reach fourscore'. 'I had a great party' he went on. 'The family— and Hazel—took me to Huntingtower. I had sandwiches and lots of whisky'. And the birth of his grandson, Peter Martin, set the seal on a happy month.

Martin Fallon had more than his fair share of sadness in his lifetime. His cruel treatment as a young boy, the family's flight to England, his initial rejection for military service, some of his isolation at Ashludie, the spiteful attacks on him when he was at Perth, his son's illness, the break-up of his marriage, all had their cumulative effect. In his old age he mellowed and became kinder. He always commanded respect, as he had done throughout his long life. He remains the first and only thoracic surgeon Tayside has ever had.

Robert Cochrane Buist

Robert Cochrane Buist

MA(Cantab), MA(St Andrews), MB, ChB(Edin), 1860–1939

Dundee in the later 19th century was at the height of its fame as a manufacturing city and its activity was generated by a number of outstanding families. Highest up the commercial hierarchy were the jute aristocracy, but not far behind were those owning the large city stores—clothing, grocery, furniture, and their like. The Buist family (Messrs R. C. Buist and Sons) had their furniture business at the top of Commercial Street from 1833 until the 1950s and with Justice's were leaders in this field. The name died with W. H. Buist—a Lord Provost—who had no family of his own to continue the firm. From this family of distinction came our first Dundee doctor.

Born in 1860 he went to the famous High School of Dundee as a boy. He proceeded to St Andrews University, where he won the Lowson, Spence and Guthrie scholarships, graduated in 1881 with first-class honours in Mathematics, and so on to Cambridge where he was senior scholar at Corpus Christi College and was fourteenth wrangler in the mathematical tripos in 1883. Now he decided to take his medical degree at Edinburgh. During his five years there he was an outstanding student, but of more significance, he began to interest himself in social causes. So he was not only captain of the university harrier club, but was one of the founders of the students' representative council, editor of the university magazine, and a student politician. At this stage of his life he began to be keenly aware of the need to do something to help the poor and lighten their burdens of long hours of toil, squalid living conditions, and high incidence of weakening and mortal disease. Though from a comfortable Dundee background, and schooled at the socially élite school there, he had not failed to notice the gulf between the West Ferry mansions of the jute Lords and the slum tenements of their workers—then amongst some of the worst in Great Britain.

It was common then—as it was until the 1940s in fact, for recent graduates to spend a period as an assistant medical officer at one of the psychiatric hospitals—lunatic asylums—and Dr Buist did a spell as an assistant at The Royal Asylum in Edinburgh. Such a short attachment brought in an income without as much hard work as an Infirmary post demanded for the tyro in medicine or surgery, and was especially sought after for this reason by those studying for a higher examination.

It was now the end of the 1880s and Dr Buist returned to Dundee. He wanted to work as an obstetrician—perhaps because of his deeply felt desire to help poor women and children. He entered this branch of medicine, which would be his professional concern for the rest of his natural life, as an assistant at the Royal Infirmary.

As schoolboy and student, R. C. Buist had shown the width of his interests, and his concern with social problems. From the early 1890s he began an interest in medical politics which continued until in due course he would become the chairman of the Scottish Council of the BMA. Bye-laws of the Dundee and District Branch of the BMA can be seen, annotated in his handwriting, of January 1894. Annual fees were then 2/6, (15 p) payable in advance. Association dues were 1 guinea *per annum*. Buist, who lived at Annfield House, was the (unnofficial) Secretary, D. M. Greig of 25 Tay Street was treasurer, J. A. C. Kynoch of 8 Airlie Place, and J. Yule Mackay of UCD—both professors in the embryo medical faculty, were active members. Early interests of the local Division were The Dundee Corporation Bill, habitual drunkards, dentists giving chloroform as an anaesthetic when not registered to do so, a dispensary for eye and ear diseases for the poor, and problems raised by chemists prescribing medicines for the public. This Dundee Branch was very new—its authorisation as a separate Branch from the Forfarshire one had been authorised by the BMA representative meeting at Newcastle-upon-Tyne on 17 November 1893. So now, the next January, its own rules were being written.

The records of 1894 have a modern ring. The President, Dr J. W. Miller, referred in his presidential address to the improved state of the profession. A Dundee Medical Society had been re-formed for the third time—the first two had failed after only a few years. The Forfarshire Medical Society was now meeting four times a year, after having only an annual meeting, with poor attendances, in the recent past. Meetings of the Dundee BMA, held in the tiny Anatomy class-room, were happy to hear of reductions in infectious diseases—including typhus—because of new public health measures. The Perth Branch—formed some years earlier than the Dundee one—invited the Dundee members of their new branch to a joint social and scientific evening. Dundee were grateful to Perth for their support and help. Thirty-five members attended the annual BMA dinner. And on 7 September 1894, the Division invited doctors from Wormit, Newport, Tayport, and St Andrews to join if they wished—train travel made for easy and quick communications in those years.

Buist was not formally appointed as honorary secretary until the AGM of 20 October. From now, he repeatedly pressed for action to help the poor of the working class. He pressed the Caledonian Railway Company 'to ensure that eye testing for their staff must be done by a properly qualified doctor if to be safely recognized.' He attacked one Friendly Society whose 'terms offered were such that no medical officer could do the work honestly' ... he noted 'the *necessity* of insurance against sickness for the working poor. If the doctor charged a fee, he had to earn it.'

61

He saw very clearly the value of social improvements in the prevention and the amelioration of disease. He saw, too, that progress would have to be continued on a national level, as doctors acting on this basis would have much more authority and so more chance of influencing government than those in a local branch. So he got appointed to the Scottish Council of the BMA, and in a few years only was elected its Chairman—in 1908. He was the Council's second Chairman. From there, he demanded social change on a national level.

In 1901 Buist was appointed lecturer in Clinical Midwifery and Gynaecology in the University of St Andrews. He taught at the Royal Infirmary and in University College in the soon-to-be-completed Medical School. This post he held until his retirement in 1925. As well as being expert in his routine work, he was early in the field of antenatal care, and studied in detail difficult positions of the child during labour and means of overcoming them. His 'Buist's pads' were such a means. They were two firm pads of oblong shape placed behind the back and shoulder of a baby lying with its face and body forwards during labour, to direct its rotation into the position of the head safest for delivery. 'Buist's pads' continued to be mentioned in obstetric textbooks till the 1950s. His 'Posture in Difficult Labour' was published in 1924 in the *BMJ*, and his correspondence with famous obstetricians on this subject continued until the 1930s.

In gynaecology, he was particularly interested in uterine cancer, as his hand-written notes on the 'Report of the Uterine Cancer Committee' in the *British Medical Journal* of 15 May 1909 showed. Early recognition he saw as the critical need. His correspondence with doctors in Edinburgh and in London continued throughout his career.

And as well as clinical problems of his specialty, he studied very carefully the results of his hospital as a whole. He collected figures of maternal morbidity and mortality, both in Dundee and in Scotland, and he used these not only for what is in the 1980s described as 'medical audit' (the politicians of that decade however saw 'audit' principally as a method of forcing hospital doctors to process more and more patients through the beds of their wards, in the pious political hope that such 'productivity' signified good medical practice; they thought medicine could be run like a grocery business)—in Buist's mind, the means of evaluating different clinical techniques by comparison and contrast of the clinical results they produced—but also to demonstrate, yet once more, that poverty led to poor obstetric performance and so had to be relieved.

This was the professional side of Buist's work. It continued not only till his retiral in 1925, but till his death 14 years later. But the other side was that of the historian, the philosopher, the academic of wide, almost renaissance-wide, activities. His range of academic interest was immense. It ranged from medical history of Dundee— 'Dundee doctors in the 16th century', 'Dr David Kinloch (Kynalochus) 1559–1617', who with the publication in 1596 of his 'De Homenes Procreatione' was probably the first Scots writer in obstetrics to have his work published, papers on Patrick Blair of the 18th century, the famous surgeon and Dundee's first-ever Fellow of the Royal Society, 'Plague Days in Dundee 1520– 1618'—to medical history in general. Here his work included *Andrew Borde, of Physycke Doctour, 1490–1549 and his Scottish Experiences*, an essay on the *Flos Medicinae* of Salerno, papers on the French physiologist and physician Laennec, and papers and articles in German. His political writings included 'Man and Society' *Parish Council Possibilities, Proagris*—an essay on the Poor Law; his philosophical *The Relativities of the Physicist and the Physician, Man and Society*; his poems and light pieces, 'Anecdotes of Isabel', 'The Soul of the Artist', 'The Enigmas of a Song'; a translation of poetry by the German humorist Fritz Renter. He was a friend of the University College library from its inception, and played a special part in the development of its medical section.

The quincentenary Festival of the University of St Andrews was in 1911. Wondrously prophetic lines adorned the title-page;

Quo fit ut omnis
Votiva pateat reluti descripta tabella
Vita senis   Horace

It was R. C. Buist who was chosen to write the chapter on medicine for 'Votiva Tabella'. No-one else, on either side of the then enlarged university, was better fitted for this task at that time.

It was perhaps his range of interests, his literary connections and the range of his academic writings, which gave Buist his unique reputation. He was a polyhist—not of the highest level, but a polyhist nonetheless. His reputation spread far beyond Dundee, and in September of 1925 the Nobel Committee for Physiology and Medicine wrote from Stockholm 'to Prof. R. Buist, asking for his nomination of a candidate for the Nobel Prize for Physiology and Medicine for 1926'. Included with the request was *The Code of Statutes of the Nobel Foundation and Special Regulations concerning prize for Physiology and Medicine*, dated 1921. There was also a list of former winners. Alas, we do not know whom he nominated—if indeed that he nominated anyone.

The strongest force in Buist's life however remained his deep-seated determination to improve the lives and prospects of the poor. He was a committed socialist. Of established religion and traditional politics of Tories and Liberals he was not enamoured. He saw his way through life at an early age—probably while a student at St Andrews. And he never lost it. Nor did he ever lose tolerance for others' views, so sympathetic was he to his fellow women and men.

In his latter years he espoused another social—public health cause; that of cremation. How much better, he agreed, that good land which could feed the people or serve as the site for new and improved housing for the poor was not wasted by being turned

64

into cemeteries of steadily increasing size. So he encouraged by verbal and written argument the establishment of a crematorium in Dundee. He was a strong member of the planning committee, later the committeee of management, and declared that his corpse would certainly be dissolved in what for him was a reliable and economical manner. He got his wish. He died on 5 February 1939.

He himself wrote the poem which was his own epitaph, and which he sent to *The Student* magazine. He called it 'Almost an Epitaph'.

Of mother born and by father trained,
Stalwart in body and not poorly brained,
Athlete and scholar, proxime accessit,
Was aught desired, he'd reach but not possess it.
Almost professor, he, full master grown,
Knew almost all men's trades and almost knew his own.
And at the end, the all-compelling Must
Made him, almost an angel, but this heap of dust.

William Fyfe Dorward

William Fyfe Dorward

BSc, MB, ChB(St Andrews), MRCGP, 1899–1964

All his patients knew him as Doctor Dorward and his students as Daddy Dorward, and these titles were always used with affection. He was born in 1899 in the schoolhouse of Kinneff in Kincardineshire, where his father was the dominie. When he was six years old the family moved to Strathmartine, near Dundee, after his father got the schoolmaster's post at Bridgefoot school.

His primary education was in his father's school. For his secondary education he went to the Morgan Academy in Dundee, at that time a great school which moulded its pupils into a characteristic Morgan Academy product recognisable for a lifetime. In 1914 he won a National Essay Competition—the prize was a sight-seeing trip to London, the then centre of Empire. The Rector gave the whole school a holiday to celebrate his success. This early introduction to London gave him a fascination for that city he never lost.

Mathematics was his strong subject at school, so much so that his father wished him to be an accountant. But his ambition as long as he could remember was for medicine. The story of his education was yet again that of the typical Scot—well aware of his father's low income, he set out to educate himself with bursaries. His family background strengthened the belief in independence and enterprise he was born with. Politically he was a staunch conservative. And so he in due course refused to allow his own four sons to apply for Education Authority grants while they were at university; they had to win his financial support by their own achievement.

To the University of St Andrews he went in 1917 with a scholarship won in open competition. First he took a BSc in Natural Sciences, followed in 1924 by his MB ChB. Once again his genetic make-up and his early childhood years in a Scottish schoolmaster's home gave him his insistence on a widely-based education. His own included Latin, German, a little Greek, but especially English literature. He had a wide knowledge of this, particularly of Shakespeare, and he used it for a range of interests from crossword puzzles to public speaking. Lowland Scots, the language of his boyhood, always remained a live language for him, and he spoke in it regularly to country and town patients. He was fluent in the Dundee patois also, understanding it perfectly but not speaking it. In his later life he was a great raconteur of Scots stories, which he shared with his kinsman Will Fyffe. He was a founder subscriber to the Scottish National Dictionary.

At St Andrews University he saw the War end. In his first summer vacation being too young for call-up he did war work as an assistant in a Forces Canteen. This took him to the Isle of Wight—for a near schoolboy a prodigious distance from home. Here he was just over the Channel from the Great War and its anxious battles of that year—1918—and saw the multitude of soldiers going and coming, to and from France. Working with him was a young conscientious objector The Hon Hugh Russell who later became the Duke of Bedford. They remained good friends, and Dr Dorward more than once defended his pacifist views although not himself agreeing with them. In the immediate post-war period he saw the numbers in the medical faculty swelled by returning ex-servicemen and like Harry Graham met some remarkable people.

Just after his graduation day his fiancée, Mary Morrison, showed him an advertisement in the Church of Scotland magazine

Life and Work. It was for a locum for Dr Herbert Torrance of Tiberias, the Scottish mission hospital beside the Lake of Galilee. (It is said that the view up the River Tay from just above the railway bridge looks like one view of the Lake of Galilee from Tiberias, and those of us who have seen this view know it to be true). Willie Dorward, as his university fellows called him, was a religious man—he applied for the job and was appointed. To Tiberias he went, to the solid stone hospital on the lakeside, with its small Church of Scotland below it. It was a part of Scotland within the Holy Land. After six months he came back to Dundee to be married and returned with his new wife Mary—by sea in those years—but not to Tiberias. Dr Torrance had returned. Dr Dorward went to Haifa, to another Scots mission hospital, this time to be doctor in charge, and stayed till 1927.

His three years in Haifa were his formative years. He was, as he said later, 'a person of importance'—being the doctor in charge of the whole hospital. Always a good linguist, he set to and became fluent in Arabic, a language most English but fewer Scots find difficult to learn. He felt that his years there lifted him out of his humble background; he got used to dealing with a range of people—including people of standing, and in turn became relaxed and confident in company. He was an ambitious young man, and was now no longer the shy rather anxious dark haired and dark-moustached student in the upper left part of the Bute photograph. Perhaps he would live out his life among the Arabs of Palestine. He met some of the few Jews there were there, but he always preferred the Arabs.

However, in 1928 he became ill with sand-fly fever, bad enough to worry him and his wife about his future health. And so he returned from the warmth and wet of Galilee, with its clear air, to the cold and wet of Dundee with its factory-made fogs.

But not immediately. He did a spell as an assistant in Forfar and a second in Streatham in London. In Streatham he enjoyed the atmosphere of a village within London and learned to dispense for the very different diseases found in a cold climate. While the Dorwards were in Streatham their first son, Morrison, was born.

These were short spells of temporary work. His next job would last the rest of his life. He bought a single-handed practice in Dundee, with as part of the package the house in Magdalen Yard Road which would be his home and his surgery—and with a view up the River Tay so like that view of the Sea of Galilee. By now it was 1931, and their second son David was born. The decade of the '30s, with the depression and the deep poverty it brought to Dundee had arrived. Most of his patients were poor—they lived in side streets between Magdalen Yard Road, Perth Road, Hawkhill and Blackness Road and mostly worked in the jute mills or the railway. Dr Dorward shared the poverty—money was scarce for him and his family too.

One day he had an idea. He would write an article for the Thomson press on a health subject, to see if by writing he could make a little more money. The article was accepted. From that time he was a regular writer for the *Topical Times*—after the *Topical Times* he was promoted to the *Peoples Journal*, and in 1939, at the start of the Second World War, he began to be 'the Doc' in the *Sunday Post*. He had to think of a subject, write the article, and submit it by Thursday for publication on Sunday. Later he ran a weekly column, also in the *Sunday Post*, called 'The Doc replies'. He kept his secret carefully and although many people and many students thought Daddy Dorward was the famous *Sunday Post* 'Doc' no-one was really sure. He continued his column till his death in 1964. Again he had followed his precepts—he had by his own efforts and hard work increased his income—and he said in his later years that it was the income from his newspaper writing that had got his four sons through university. Douglas, his third, was born in 1933, and Ian, the youngest, in 1936. A Dundee wifie, knowing how much he had hoped for a daughter, said, with real Dundee perception and kindly humour 'The doctor's filled his hoose wi' laddies looking for a lassie'.

Douglas Dorward's birth made him look for another source of extra income. In 1933 the post of Police Surgeon in Dundee fell vacant. He had had no training whatever in forensic work, but undaunted he applied. His application was successful. So he entered the third part of his trio of life activities—family doctoring, writing for profit, and now police surgeon's work.

In 1933 the facilities for investigation of crime by a police surgeon were primitive by modern standards. The only chemical tests available in Dundee were for blood and seminal fluid. Technology as known today simply did not exist. Examination of tissues by microscopic examination was well recognized, and well developed by experts in large centres—London and Glasgow. As always Edinburgh University was ahead of the field in having a long-established department in its medical faculty. But Dr Dorward was not a trained pathologist. His predecessor Dr Lennox was dead, so was in no position to advise. He was going to have to learn 'on the job'.

He quickly did two things. First he got the police to build a new post-mortem room for police work, next to the headquarters in Bell Street. Next he sought help from the established men— Glaister of Glasgow, Sydney Smith of Edinburgh and most of all James Webster, whom he had known at St Andrews. James Webster was already making a name for himself in London. In due course he would succeed Spilsbury as Chief Home Office Pathologist and become one of the major St Andrews graduates of the century. And after a year or two he got Dr George Smith, a young pathologist in Dundee, to do his microscopic work for him. George Smith remained his local colleague until Dr Dorward's death, and would willingly help with difficult P.M. examinations.

'What sort of mortuary do you want?' said the Chief Constable. 'I want one with a coal fire' he replied. He wanted this to burn unwanted pieces of tissue, and also so that he could burn coffee in a big shovel to mask the often unpleasant smells. (Every year, groups of students, three at a time, were present at a police post-mortem while doing their university course in forensic medicine. 'I think we could do with some coffee' Daddy Dorward would say to Brown, his assistant. The students would relax a little—they were invariably rather tense and ill-at-ease during these often unpleasant procedures—but their expectations were dashed when Mr Brown came along with a large shovel, poured ground coffee beans all over it—held it over the fire till it smoked, and then brandished it in the four corners of the room like an incense burner).

The stocky, solid Will Brown was Daddy Dorward's mortuary attendant over many years. Never clever enough to be a police constable, his previous job had been to drive around on his motor bicycle and clean police boxes. Once he was driving up to the police box in Dudhope Terrace when he saw three boys running out of a house where they had been stealing apples. A fourth, very small boy was standing nearby, clearly an accomplice. Bill Brown leapt off his bicycle, seized him, and interrogated him severely as to the names of the older boys. Tearfully he denied all knowledge of their names, insisting he was an innocent bystander. Mr Brown thought a short period of detention would change his attitude, so locked him in the police box while he did another job. After fifteen minutes he came back. The little boy was still tearful and sad. Mr Brown let him go. As soon as he was ten yards away he turned and shouted 'Eh ken a' their names. They stealt the aipples. And whit's mair, E've ate yer piece'. Then he was off, running as hard as his legs would go.

Dr Dorward's work was not confined to police post-mortem examinations. He was responsible for the routine medical examination of police—both recruits and those in service. He also examined any prisoner ill in his cell. He was also responsible, under the law as it existed at the time, for the medical examination of those brought in by the police who were thought to be under the influence of drink while driving. During his years as police surgeon in Dundee there were no blood alcohol estimations, no breathalyser. He was a life long teetotaller, and regarded drink and driving—rightly—as a most serious offence. He devised his own system of tests for those charged—walking along a straight line, co-ordination tests of other sorts, balancing tests, as well as verbal questioning. These he described in great detail to his student classes. They were not always totally sympathetic.

While doing post-mortem examinations in road accident victims, he would open the stomach carefully, and put his nose inside and smell. Though he had a keen nose for alcohol, he was less accurate in diagnosing the particular drink taken. Will Brown was always asked to sniff the stomach content too, and he often more accurately diagnosed beer when the police surgeon had diagnosed whisky!

The Dorwards continued their friendship with the Torrance family of Tiberias. Dr Torrance sent his two daughters to a boarding school in England, and Dr Dorward regularly had them up to Dundee for Christmas holidays. His sons played with them as children, and Morrison, his eldest, met Lydia Torrance, later to be his wife, when he was ten years old and she eight.

The forensic work was now a large and important interest. He constantly worked to learn more of this branch of medicine, and was in regular touch with Professsor Sydney Smith and Dr Keith Simpson of London, as well as with Sir James Webster. This was vital, as he had no background of knowledge of the more scientific sort to build upon. It was vital, too, for his work as lecturer in Forensic Medicine and Toxicology at the University of St Andrews. This was a Degree Examination, part of the 'Third Professional Examination for the Degrees of MB ChB in the University of St Andrews' and was taken in the fourth year of study, together with Public Health.

His university department had also to be built from scratch. He had accommodation in the old medical school building in University College in association with the Public Health department—a single rather dull brown room on the first floor. He was in effect 'under' the Public Health Department—he also taught vaccination—and relations with Dr Burgess, the MOH, later Professor Burgess, CBE were good. He did not unfortunately get on so well with Professor Alex. Mair, Professor Burgess' successor, but eventually they learned to agree, or agree to differ if the occasion arose.

He had great pride in being a member of university staff in his own medical school, and took a great interest in his students . His rather gruff voice was remembered by all—his great phrases—'take the bull by the horns' in cases of rape—'wear a dark suit' when in the witness box, to maintain the good name of the medical profession—'the questions requirin' to be answered in the case of a boady recovered from water'—the first of which was 'was the body dead or not' (this provoked applause). He also advised the expert medical witness to face slightly away from the advocate questioning him, so that he had a second or two longer, while turning towards him to answer, to work out what to say. This did him no help himself at some trials—notably the trial of the Indian seaman accused of murdering a Dundee man in the Stannergate in 1950, when he was sharply cross-examined by Sir John Cameron, Dean of the Faculty of Advocates, later Lord Cameron, for the defence. Political considerations at the time of the trial had ensured this high-ranking defence counsel. Undertones of homosexuality—a novelty in the Dundee of the day—were also whispered. This was one of the many cases where George Smith's evidence as a trained pathologist was vital—when he came back from Dunkirk and was invalided out of the Army, George Smith did more and more in this part of the police work.

Dr Dorward's love of Shakespeare led him to prepare a lecture, which he gave to each year of law students taking his Forensic Medicine course, on the medico-legal aspects of the murders which occurred in Shakespeare's plays. Once he set a class examination for law students which consisted of quotations from Shakespeare referring to various illness, injury and death, and required the

74

candidates to write comments on these quotations. He considered that all law students, as properly educated men and women, ought to be familiar with Shakespeare's works. Not all were, and he caused some irritation and worry to them by this whimsy.

Daddy Dorward used often to remark that he would have liked to go on the stage. His two new posts certainly furnished him with regular public appearances both in the lecture theatre and in the sheriff court. His family grew to know by his mood how receptive his students had been that day in response to his tales or whether the defence counsel had caught him out. He was very sensitive to the mood of an audience, and loved public speaking as a challenge he enjoyed. He spoke regularly at Rotary Clubs. He was a founder member of Dundee Repertory Theatre in 1939, attending its very first production *Hassan* by Elroy Flecker and virtually all its subsequent ones. He took an immense interest in the Dundee Theatre—was on the Board of Directors, medical officer to the staff and successive casts, and took guests to plays at all possible occasions.

The third part of his life—his work as a family doctor—was the dearest and greatest to him. He loved his patients, and spent endless time with them. He remained single-handed, with no time off, no free weekends, till 1944. Then the ever heavier work-load of the war caused him to take his first assistant. This was Dr Sheila Conacher. But he was reluctant to delegate responsibility and work. Dr Conacher lived with the Dorward family, and every evening after supper he would go over all the patients she had seen, question her on what she had said, diagnosed and prescribed, and these case conferences remained a regular feature of the practice, continuing often till after midnight. (One trainee after the war was told on his first day with the Dorward practice at the end of the evening surgery 'I'll see you at 8 o'clock'. When he appeared bright and smiling at 8 the next morning, the error of his ways was explained). They were rather hard-going for younger doctors, and even his son, Dr Morrison Dorward, confessed years

75

later that he 'groaned a bit' after he joined the practice himself in 1955 after leaving the Army and was obliged to sit till 1 o'clock in the morning, when he wanted only to get home to his own young wife and family. His other partner, Dr Priscilla Turnbull, had joined the practice in 1953 as a trainee—she and Morrison both became partners in 1956.

As well as all this staggering amount of work—which the diary he kept described in such detail—he created time for other interests. He was a bee-keeper, and took delight in giving honey to patients. He wrote articles on the subject. He loved bird watching. On Sundays, when he used to visit older patients, especially country ones, he would stop to look at birds. Wax-wings were a favourite species, and when they arrived in the country near Dundee each late winter, or to their regular haunts on the cotoneasters in Ancrum Road School, he would come home full of excitement at the first sighting.

Flowers too enthralled him. He taught himself to paint wild flowers, starting by water-colouring the line drawings in a botanical field-book, and then with practice directly from nature. He knew the places in the town where special flowers or trees grew, and he would watch for their coming into bloom, year by year. A particular one was the sycamore tree growing just west of the Morgan Tower Pharmacy in the University garden. It had an unusual, very early, yellowish-green leafage. He called it the 'Gregory's Mixture' tree.

A character like this—for he was a *character*—had many, many stories recounted about what he said or did. Some related to his total absorption with the patient he was dealing with at the particular moment. 'I don't want to keep you too long, Dr Dorward' said one man with a problem. 'There are so many people outside waiting '. 'I am speaking with you just now' the doctor replied, 'and I will speak to you as long as need be. If they need to see me, they will wait. If they do not really need me, they will go home'. This was long before the days of the appointment

76

system. To a middle-aged man he said 'Your age has nothing to do with numbers'—and the man said, twenty five years later, how that remark had kept him young well into his seventies.

His strong teetotalism sometimes provoked comment. At a mens' club talk he was giving, about his life as a GP and police surgeon, an aggressive questioner demanded: 'Doctor Dorward—you're a teetotaler. How can you dare to examine motorists charged with drinking and driving if you never drink yourself?' 'If I have to go to the police staion to examine a man charged with drinking and driving', he replied, 'and I've had three doubles myself, and arrive at the station unsteady on my feet, what sort of opinion will the police—and the prisoner—have of me when I examine him?' He was the only Dundee police surgeon at the time.

Some thought him too strict, too strongly antagonistic to drink. The changed attitudes of the later 1980s would not have thought so. When he died, in 1964, he was in his last year of Presidency of the Police Surgeons' Federation of Great Britain and Northern Ireland—the proudest achievement of his life. And he died as he had lived, in post.

The story that the streets of Dundee were lined with mourners as his coffin passed was true. As the hearse passed along Magdalen Yard Road, grown men wept openly. No provost, no professor, no jute lord, no local politician earned such public grief. And at every major road crossing, the cortege was saluted by an immaculate police constable, posted there to ensure the smooth progress of his last journey. 'There were more flowers at the crematorium', said one man who knew Dundee well, 'than I ever saw before or since'.

Walter Gordon Campbell

Walter Gordon Campbell

VRD, LDS, MB, ChM(St Andrews), FRCSEng, FRCSEdin, 1907–1981

Walter Campbell came from a Dundee dental family of distinction. His grandfather, also Walter LDS (1828–1919) had two sons— Graham Campbell and Henry Gordon Campbell. They were dentists in the city, and when the dental hospital was opened before the First World War, Graham and Henry who was known as Gordon, were in turn leaders of the school which the University of St Andrews soon founded. Regulations for it were put before the Faculty of Medicine of St Andrews University on 25 January 1916 and Dr Graham Campbell became the first Dean. Years later Henry Gordon Campbell, Walter Campbell's father, was appointed by St Andrews as the first Professor of Dental Surgery in Scotland.

Our Walter Campbell was born on 3 March 1907. He was educated first locally at the High School of Dundee, but left to finish his education at Ipswich School, Suffolk. He was first an LDS of St Andrews then MB ChB in 1929. He continued his training after graduation at the Middlesex and St Bartholomew's Hospitals in London. In 1933 he took the final examination for the Fellowship of the Royal College of Surgeons of England. In October 1935 he was appointed to Dundee Royal as assistant surgeon and as the only local man there with the 'English Fellowship'.

His early life was that of a boy of the times who came from a professional family background—comfortable, settled and happy. But like so many of his contemporaries—no matter what their social background—he became ill with tuberculosis of the glands of his neck. This form of the disease was common because milk was infected with the *tubercle bacillus*—and there was no pasteurisation locally. Like so many, he 'had his neck glands cut', and then spent summer convalescing in the country parts of the Carse of Gowrie. Much later in his life he recalled sitting in the shelter of the Sidlaws and looking down to the evening sun on the River Tay, and the warmth which helped him to feel well and strong again.

While a student he was briefly a member of the University Officers' Training Corps, but he left this to join the Tay Division of the Royal Naval Volunteer Reserve. The Navy remained a life-long interest. He boxed in Naval boxing competitions, and his broken nose dated from these encounters. His boxing prowess stood him in good stead one summer when he went to sea in an Arbroath fishing boat. The weather was bad, the catch pathetically poor, and some of the crew turned on him, declaring him a Jonah because of his fair hair and seeking to blame him for their own fear and failure. He gave better than he got, and his tormentors retreated in disorder. From that hour, perhaps, came the strong jaw, the determined look in the blue eyes, so characteristic of Walter Campbell throughout his life. Those eyes could sparkle and dance with fun and delight like the sea on a summer's day. They could be cool and placid like a still calm. They could be angry and threatening, like a rising sea, and they could rarely blaze with anger like a fierce storm. But no matter how fierce the rage of the storm had been, the even blue returned once the waves settled, and whatever had happened was put by and forgotten.

After his first house jobs in 1929 with Prof. Price and 1930 with Prof. Patrick, he went to Liverpool as a surgical trainee in 1931. At the 'Liverpool Southern' he learned orthopaedic surgery, and made a special study of x-rays. One of his chiefs, Mr Armour, had known and worked with the great Sir Robert Jones of Oswestry. It was now began his fascination for orthopaedic surgery. In Liverpool of those years there was a vast amount of clinical experience available—greater than he could ever have gained in Dundee.

But the call of the River Tay brought Walter back to Scotland, and he took up a 6 month surgical post in the Royal Infirmary at Perth. Perth was another city he enjoyed, though the work as resident surgical officer there was hard—he the only assistant, on duty every night, with one half day off each week—and this half day ended about 10.00 p.m. when he went back on call. One early evening he did a very difficult appendix operation, and left the Infirmary to walk along the river by the North Inch. Suddenly a panic seized him; he had cut an important nerve, supplying vital muscles in the leg. He rushed back the mile and a half's slope from the riverside to the hospital, and dashed breathless into the ward. To his huge relief, the patient could straighten his knee. The nerve was undamaged.

His Dundee Royal Infirmary post was a more senior one, though he was still responsible for emergencies. Now he had students to teach, and his teaching was clear but sometimes in the recollection of those he taught, too sharp, and his criticisms too severe, for their comfort. These were the days when medical students were questioned sharply, sometimes with hostility and sarcasm, by their tutors, By now, too, his special interest in orthopaedic surgery was progressing, and now his questioning acute brain began to try and test methods of management based on conceptions he had made while visiting the continent.

In 1936 he married. His bride Nancy Isabelle Rait, daughter of Lieutenant Colonel J. W. F. Rait, of the Indian Medical Service. Her mother was Isabella Boyd and her uncle, William Boyd, was Chairman of the Dundee Dental Hospital.   So began a marriage of great happiness, happiness for Walter and Nancy, and also happiness between the older generations and the younger.

81

By 1939 he had become Principle Medical Officer to the Tay Division of the RNVR, and been promoted Lieutenant-Commander. As a volunteer reservist he was called up for service in the summer of 1939 before actual outbreak of war. His very first job was to examine recruits in the submarine depot ship at anchor in the Tay, HMS *Forth*, but he soon found himself in Portsmouth and on his first evening in the wardroom was agog with excitement. Next morning at early breakfast he was most impressed to find that every officer had a rating standing behind him at table who, as he later recalled 'buttered your toast for you and put the marmalade on'. He was told by the senior medical officer that as the most recently-arrived junior he would have to take the venereal disease sick parade that afternoon. To his surprise—and some alarm—he discovered that many of the attenders he had already seen—acting as mess waiters the same morning!

In October, just after hostilities had begun, he was posted to London to help fit out the Bibby liner *Oxfordshire* before it set sail for Sierra Leone in West Africa as a hospital ship on 11 November 1939. The only people on board on the voyage out were specialists like himself and there was very little work. He remained at Freetown until 1941. Before the war really burst into action with the German invasion of France, Nancy had gone out to join him in the April and had stayed until she returned in the S.S. *Strathaird* in February 1941. From October to December 1941, he was back in Chatham awaiting his next posting. He was disappointed to find himself ordered to Skegness, to the shore establishment HMS *Royal Arthur*—a commandeered Butlin's holiday camp. Here he made the best of his time by studying the repair of herniae—a common operation amongst young ratings—and it was here he devised his own method of repair.

His next assignment was to South Africa, then part of the world-wide British Empire, and to the naval base at Simonstown in July 1944, on the busy sea-route to the Middle East, India, and the war in the Far East. His surgical chief there was a fervid rugby enthusiast who forced him to watch not one but often two rugby matches every Saturday, as well as evening or afternoon games throughout the week. When he returned home at the end of the war, he vowed he would never watch a rugby match again!

While working in Dundee Royal Infirmary Casualty in 1934 and 1935, he had begun to test his hypotheses on nervous system reflexes and on the use of local anaesthesia in sprains and bony injuries not only to relieve pain but to quicken healing. He described the relief of swelling of the injured part after pain relief, and the corresponding acceleration in healing. In this he anticipated the free use of ultrasound, 30 years later, in allowing soldiers on street patrol in Belfast to have a sprained ankle relieved in days or even hours. His ChM thesis on 'Physiological Rest and the Relief of Pain' was sent to St Andrews during the war, and was accepted in 1943, with commendation.

At the end of the war, Lieutenant Commander Campbell was demobilised promptly, and he was required to return to Dundee to take up his post again as an assistant surgeon. He became junior to Mr John Robb in the Royal Infirmary. In 1948 came the National Health Service and he found himself promoted to the new rank of consultant. Still as assistant he was well down the pecking order: Dr G. R. Tudhope sent him packing from the post-mortem room one day in the summer of 1948 in no uncertain manner because of a wrong diagnosis on the death of a patient. And even when he became the 'chief' on wards 13 and 14 in the old Caird Block of DRI later that year after the sudden death of Mr Robb, he could still find himself at the wrong end of blistering criticism by the professor of the day, Professor Sonny Alexander.

Yet he was steadily increasing his standing and his status. He moved into his beautiful red stone home in Farington Terrace, and had a direct telephone line installed between it and Fernbrae Nursing Home next door on the Perth Road. His zeal for fine cars began to be indulged, and students climbing the hill from the

83

D

Infirmary to the William Low Residence in Dudhope Terrace at lunch-time would see his Bentley car heading westwards, his characteristic chin jutting out as he drove, his hat firmly on his head.

In 1951 he suffered what seemed to be a heart attack, a collapse, a period off work, but then recovery. This recovery seemed to coincide with a gentler manner to his students and also his staff, and, perhaps, a softening of his character to the amiable yet firm decisiveness which his colleagues and especially his junior staff would always recall.

Early 1952 brought a great change in Walter Campbell's clinical charge. The University of St Andrews had a great plan envisaged in its Court's comments on the Goodenough Report of 1943, to extend and develop its medical faculty in the post-war years, and a feature of this far-seeing development was the institution of a range of specialist departments. Mr Ian Smillie, the orthopaedic surgeon who had worked so wonderfully at Larbert in the war-time Emergency Medical Service, was appointed by the University as its specialist orthopaedic surgeon. He had already been lecturing for some 3 years. His main unit was the huge, 250–bed one at Bridge of Earn Hospital in Perthshire, but he was to be given charge of wards 13 and 14 as his DRI base. Just before him, had arrived the first full-time Professor of Surgery in St Andrews, Donald M. Douglas, from Edinburgh in October of 1951. As a result of these major changes, Walter Campbell and his unit were transferred to Maryfield Hospital.

He had in fact applied for the orthopaedic post Mr Smillie had just won. This was a disappointment to him, as he loved orthopaedics and saw at once that this branch of surgery would now be denied to him forever. Just before the appointment was advertised, Walter Campbell had been asked by the *Lancet* to review a book of Mr Smillie's. He had done this, including some criticism, and not adding his name, as was then the custom. By some it was said, entirely unfairly, that his criticism had been because of his failure to obtain the orthopaedic post. The report and its aftermath became a *cause célèbre*. As a result, *Lancet* reviews were from then on never anonymous, but had the name of the reviewer always seen.

He had some reservations about the move to Maryfield. Maryfield was the old city hospital of Dundee, the hospital for the grim-walled poorhouse. Although Professor Charteris, Professor of Materia Medica at the University of St Andrews, had looked after patients there, and although there were specialist surgical, maternity, and even psychiatric wards, the hospital had not the status enjoyed by Dundee Royal. There was, for example, no out-patient department, and there was no laboratory. But the University, as part of its carefully thought out plan for extending student teaching in the post-war years was intent on up-grading Maryfield to the position of the second teaching hospital in Dundee. So at the same time as Mr Campbell, there moved to Maryfield Professor Ian Hill, the new Professor of Medicine, Miss Jean Herring the Obstetrician, and Dr George Smith the Pathologist. Professor A. D. Hitchin, Professor of Dental Surgery and successor to his own father, was also to undertake care of dental patients, and Professor Anthony Ritchie of the Bute Medical Department, St Salvator's College, was appointed a visiting consultant in diseases of the nervous system. Unlike Dundee Royal, Maryfield boasted a staff name board, where the names of the senior (and junior) staff were displayed, and whether they were IN or OUT. All these joined Professor R. B. Hunter already established in his Therapeutics Unit.

To increase the size of his potential surgical practice, Mr Campbell was appointed consultant surgeon at Blairgowrie and Meigle Cottage Hospitals—where he would see out-patients and operate, and because of the mental disease unit at Maryfield, he had an appointment also as consulting surgeon to Westgreen Hospital at Liff. Mr James Kinnear, who had earlier become a consultant surgeon in wards 13 and 14 after the death of Mr John

85

Robb was appointed in order to assist Mr Campbell in this work.

At first the main drive in Maryfield came from the ambition and flair of Professor R. B. Hunter, who was determined to have a Department of Therapeutics so good that it would rival and excel the traditionally senior Department of Medicine. But the Department of Professor Hill at once took up the challenge, and two new physicians of great promise, Dr John Stowers an expert in treatment of diabetes, and Dr Kenneth Lowe, an expert in the new cardiology, who had also worked at the Hammersmith Hospital in London on the first British artificial kidney were appointed in the summer of 1952. But while these two departments pursued their rivalry, the 'surgical service' as Walter Campbell decided to call it, was the one and only and so was assured of a huge load of surgical work for teaching and training.

For 8 years he worked prodigiously hard. His skill was astonishing, his speed of operating became legendary. His repertoire was as wide as Mr Frank Brown's, for he too carried out cerebral leucotomy for mental patients—exceeded only by Mr Brown's enterprise in doing the first cardiac surgery in Dundee. These were the years when a surgeon of skill and resource could still cover a wide field—surgery of the head and neck, breast, abdomen and of the urinary system, now called Urology. It was especially in his attitude to the minutiae of surgical technique that he concentrated his considerable talents for innovation. After the retiral of Mr Brown, his status increased further. He was by seniority the senior surgical chief in the district—senior to the professor, Donald Douglas. He determined that he would maintain that place and not lose it by default.

He loved to operate. His speed was remarkable—he could remove three quarters of a stomach in 35 minutes, completing the joining of the remnant to the bowel below with the flowing needle strokes, as he sewed the anastomosis, of a master craftsman. He could remove a rectal tumour, all alone, in just over an hour. He looked always for technical perfection. He would show and teach his registrars all his discoveries—the extra cut here, the bevelled edge there, the precise way to hold the various needles as they were pushed through the whole range of tissues from bowel lining to skin surface. He had that unique quality only the greatest surgeons possess, of knowing exactly what the essential steps in a procedure were, and how to complete them quickly and safely. His hands performed no unnecessary dissection, no irrelevant manipulation. His registrars could not but learn from such a craftsman. Their only loss, perhaps, was that his technical interest and ability made him sometimes think of mechanical solutions rather than physiological, functional ones.

But it was not simply repetitive surgery. His thoughts and ideas for new anatomical approaches, different use of stitches, new operations, research projects, were full of challenging thought. He obtained a research room in the newly built clinical investigation unit, and encouraged his staff to study antibiotic resistance, palliative surgery in cancer, slipperiness of human fat, surgery of renal dialysis, techniques in the developing specialty of Intensive Care, and even electron microscopy. He thought ahead to the problems of organ transplantation, and looked forward to the time when it would become a standard practice. In the Fellowship examination, he was equally at home asking candidates how to disarticulate a hip as how to construct a pedicle skin graft. In his now considerable private practice, he willed his patients better. His confidence bred success. Even with a bad result he seemed always in command, and he knew how to cap final success. One prostatectomy patient of his in Fernbrae lay for 3 weeks with a wound leakage. The day after it closed, he 'phoned the patient's wife. 'You can open the champagne now' he told her as he passed on the good news. And then, in 1969, at the age of 62, he retired from his Dundee practice. Very far-seeing, he sensed the way the National Health Service was moving, and was not surprised when the army of line managers and administrative medical officers appeared 4 years later.

87

He had enjoyed not only his work, but also his recreations—his shooting which he loved so much, his occasional golf, his music. And he left the River Tay and Scotland for the Swan River and Western Australia. He left Ballindean, his beautiful mansion in the Carse of Gowrie near Inchture. He left his shooting, his membership of the Royal and Ancient Club of St Andrews, of the Eastern Club in Dundee, of Lloyds of London, of the Association of Surgeons while that association was still an élite. He left his devoted ward staff—Sister Welsh and Sister Stobie, and his devoted theatre sisters, Sister Roy and later Sister Butchart. He left his wonderfully devoted secretary, Mabel MacDonald—'you clever thing' as he used to say to her. On the other side of the world would be his son Douglas. His daughters Sheila and Mary were now married and living in Eastern and Western Canada.

They emigrated to Perth, Western Australia where they stayed 6 months but found it too hot so joined Douglas in Albany, a coastal town 250 miles south. Once again his keen intelligence, his drive and his cheerful enterprise were there for all to see. There was an acute shortage of doctors in Queensland, so began a 3 month job at a bush town Baralaba 100 miles from Rockhampton in April 1971. 'Matron there was wonderful' said Mrs Campbell later. 'Walter was a bit of a cheat doing GP work and she and *all* the other matrons to follow him across Australia, kept him right'.

He returned to Albany and undertook locums for the West Australian Medical Board, bringing him in contact with the Royal Flying Doctor Service. He worked at Exmouth, Onslow, Carnarvon, Dampier, Broome and Meekatharra Hospitals. As ever he was in his element, the thrill of the Flying Doctor Service (though laughingly and modestly referred to as: 'not as romantic as you might think, just like a clinic at Meigle or Blair'), the challenge of surgery in the outback where his amazing technical skill and speed was so valuable in often primitive conditions, filled him with the joy of an operation neatly done and the patient relieved.

88

In Albany with his son Douglas he became a farmer. The Campbells started the first Lincoln Red cattle farm in Western Australia. Yet once more the draw of surgery which he so loved induced him to return to active practice. He still found time to do consultant surgery when asked by local doctors and general practice surgery in the bush an hour and a half away at Jerramungup. He retired in 1979, after being in practice 50 years.

He did not forget the medical school his family had served with such distinction. His will provided money to endow a Walter Gordon Campbell prize for a St Andrews graduate at Manchester as a senior medical student, and for a Dundee senior medical student. This prize was to be awarded yearly to a student showing 'special aptitude for surgery'.

A special aptitude for surgery was exactly what Walter Campbell had. He was of his age—a graduate at a time when technical skill was all-important. Anaesthesia and biochemical control were less developed in his formative years than they became in his maturity. His obituary in the *British Medical Journal* of 25 April 1981 expressed the love and respect his apprentices had felt for him, and for his so-happy family and marriage. It read:—
'Walter Gordon Campbell died 30 March 1981. He worked his staff hard, but rewarded them with his affection, trust and loyalty. Ambition, envy, and criticism of colleagues were not of his nature, and he had no interest in committees, conferences, colleges or medical politics. Only pretentiousness, expendiency, and disloyalty angered him and aroused a cool contempt. Because ambition had little interest for him, he sometimes appeared a little aloof, but this concealed his humility and shyness. For those of us who worked wih him, and were taught by him, there will always be only one surgical chief'.

Walter would have been proud of his nine grandchildren currently living in Britain, Canada and Australia and pleased that the medical tradition is being continued in the family. His daughter Sheila had a medical degree from Edinburgh and her son

89

Michael hopes to graduate in Medicine in 1990 from Queen's University, Kingston, Ontario, Canada; another son Christopher has his PhD in Physics from Lavel University, Quebec City, Canada.

Jean Herring

Dr Jean Herring

BSc, MB, ChB(St Andrews), FRCSEd, FRCOG

Our next doctor is unique in two respects. First, she is our only lady. But second, she must be the only senior hospital doctor about whom no-one has ever made an unkind remark.

She was born in Edinburgh, grew up in St Andrews and went to St Katharines and St Leonards Schools there. She went as a day girl, as her home was that of Professor Herring, the Chandos Professor of Physiology in the university. As long as she could remember she wanted to be a doctor. While at school she remembered Dr Brown, a lady medical missionary from Ludhiana in India coming to give a talk to the university women—and she remembered the red gowns of the students who came to this special lecture. She was so deeply impressed by it that she never forgot it—as a result she felt she wanted to be a medical missionary herself.

School was followed by university. She took a BSc in 1930, remembering Dr Hynd the biochemistry lecturer as kindly— medical students on the other hand remembered him as severe. This was because the pure science students he knew were taking his class from interest, but he knew equally that the medicals were taking it because they had to, and their interest in his subject was often less than ecstatic.

'There were only about 10 local people in our year', Miss Herring recalled. 'The others—over 20—were from overseas. I

dissected with Francis Ibiam, from Nigeria, one of the first if not
the first African student in Medicine. He became Sir Francis but
gave up his knighthood later after some annoyance in the Nigerian
civil war'. She remembered particularly how kind the professors
were to Francis Ibiam—Professor Waterston of Anatomy said to
him at the dissecting table: 'People here with pink skins have black
lungs from the coal and dust they breathe in. You have black skin,
but coming from where you do, your lungs will be lovely and
pink'.

Most of her medical year were from the United States. 'We
heard that 20 American Jews were coming over', she said. 'We
were all a bit apprehensive, and I remember my father looking
alarmed when the whole 20 of them kept following him around.
But we found them very adaptable.'

St Andrews was early in its acceptance of women students. Miss
Herring recalls Professor Price 'I was a great admirer of Professor
Price—in fact I rather hero-worshipped him—he had been so kind
to me, when as a child I was under his care' and his double clinics
for 3rd and 5th year students—'with the six of us women sitting in
the front row. It was a thrill to be beckoned out to examine a
case, and he pulled our legs unmercifully, but with a great sense of
fun.'

For as happened in those times, half the medical year began at
St Andrews and a smaller half began at Dundee. The smaller
Dundee numbers were made up by the dental students there. The
St Salvator's College contingent crossed to Dundee in their third
year, and the combined group then began clinical training at
Dundee Royal Infirmary. Jean Herring made the move with her
friends from The Bute and graduated MB ChB in 1933. Her class
performances earned her one of the house doctor's posts in the
Infirmary, and she was a house physician on wards 2 and 5 with
Professor Charteris, the Professor of Materia Medica who had
come from Glasgow, and with Dr A. R. Moodie who was in
charge of the Eye Department.

She thought she would like to move away from Tayside—where she had spent her life so far—and applied for a house surgeon's job about as far away as she could—at Bristol. After she was appointed she learned that another girl resident working there had got her the job—'not my merits as I'd thought!' The senior surgeon had handed the bunch of applications to his deputy to choose one—he did not bother himself. He in turn tossed them to his house physician, who was a girl, a Rhodes Scholar from what was then Southern Rhodesia, called Isobel Russell, an Edinburgh graduate. 'Pick another woman if there is one' he said. 'You're lonely here.' Female house surgeons were extremely rare in 1934 and she felt lucky to be chosen. The post covered all branches of surgery including orthopaedics, and Jean was not spared by her seniors. Happily the two girls remained life-long friends—Dr Isobel is now retired and lives in Capetown.

But her connections helped her next appointment. Professor Cappell of Pathology knew how difficult it was for outsiders to be appointed to a post of any sort in Glasgow, and how tight the Glasgow mafia was. 'He *helped* me land a plum job.' This was at the Royal Hospital for Sick Children. But after six months, Jean Herring needed no sponsor for her next—at the Royal Maternity Woman's Hospital. Everyone had got to know how good she was. This was a key job in her life—she learned much from the great volume of maternity that hospital passed through its wards, but also from its great variety and the enormous difficulties in labour and pregnancy suffered by the Glasgow poor in those later years of the depression. It was here, perhaps, that her inbred kindness and sincerity of character developed into the unique kindness and never-ending courtesy of her mature years.

It was 1936 and she moved for a spell to Birmingham as locum assistant Medical Officer of Health for Maternity and Child Welfare. Her aim was still to be a family doctor; Dr Bobby Mathers, the ENT chief at DRI whom she respected and liked, told her 'a good general practitioner is the very best of doctors'.

And then came the order which shaped her career. It was from Margaret Fairlie, the obstetrician at DRI, and her senior by half a generation, *and* whom she always referred to—even when she had been retired for 20 years—as 'Doctor Fairlie'. She said to Jean Herring 'Get your FRCS and then we'll see'. And so—such was respect for seniority in those years—she went to Edinburgh, took the Fellowship course for 5 months, and duly became a Fellow of the Royal College of Surgeons. She took obstetrics as her special subject.

Back to Dundee and she found herself put up as a candidate for the DRI post of assistant obstetrician and gynaecologist. 'What will I say' she asked Margaret Fairlie, 'if they ask about gynaecology at the interview. I haven't done any.' 'Don't worry' replied the Madam. 'They'll all be men and they'd be so embarrassed (at the mention of *gynaecology*) they'd go under the table.' The interview was in the Board Room of what was then the Trustee Savings Bank (it is now part of Dundee High School). When she came in, young Miss Herring found a room full of black coated elderly men. They stood up courteously as she entered. They were obviously on their best behaviour. A lady candidate for a senior hospital appointment had only once come their way—and that was Dr Margaret Fairlie herself.

As soon as appointed, Dr Jean found herself a spectator in the disagreement then raging between the University and the DRI Board of Governors over the appointment of a new Professor of Obstetrics and Gynaecology—a successor to Professor McGibbon. 'There was no prof. when I arrived and I had to read Professor McGibbon's lectures. It must have been awfully boring but they were good lectures.' The difficulty was resolved when Dr Margaret Fairlie, MB, ChB, was appointed to the chair.

Now Dr Jean's career really began. Her immediate academic requirement was to pass the Membership examination of the Royal College of Obstetricians and Gynaecologists. Once again—by her own account—she was *fortunate* in being examined by a senior chief from Manchester who had known Dr Fairlie when she herself was training there. It seems more certain that her own obvious knowledge and skill earned her, her pass. Later, in 1951, she became a Fellow of the College.

1939 followed and the war started. Her status grew with her experience and skill in obstetrics. As the war progressed, more women appeared on the scene, but there were only two at senior level—Dr Jean Herring and Professor Margaret Fairlie. It was largely from Professor Fairlie that she learned gynaecology—the younger respected the older greatly. Dr Fairlie had learned to operate from Professor Price and in St Mary's Hospital in Manchester. Each lady assisted the other with private patients in the small nursing homes then scattered around Dundee, and the Madam taught her now number two. Dr Chisholm ('Chis' as Dr Jean always called him affectionately) was in DRI at that time, and 'he was nice too'. Disappointed in his failure to get the Chair he had hoped for, he moved to Maryfield to become the Chief there.

She continued to lecture and to examine both students and midwives. But her 'war work' included medical examinations of girls joining the women's Services. 'My examining meant I'd to give up students some times. Once I found I'd arranged to examine a bunch of recruits and give a lecture at the same time. I decided I'd have to do the examinations so just did not go to the lecture and never told anyone.' 'At the start the standards were very high. All their teeth had to meet and be there. But standards fell later.' The years were hard and she like others was glad when Dr Sandy Buchan was appointed lecturer after the end of the war—a welcome addition to the staff. During the war Dr Willie Kinnear left for service and asked Jean to take over the secretaryship of the Dundee Branch of the BMA for him. This she did throughout the war years and as secretary she attended the only BMA Annual Representative Meeting to be held in wartime. This was in September 1942, when there was a lull in the bombing

97

of London. London she remembered for the isolated beauty of St Paul's, splendid among the devastation around,—and for the endless number of American servicemen who seemed to be everywhere!

After 12 years at the Royal Infirmary she was moved to Maryfield—but now as the Chief. 'It was promotion but Dr Fairlie came around regularly.' Miss Jean Herring was one of several senior clinicians 'posted' to the old Poor Law Hospital to develop it under St Andrews University's plan. She stopped her formal student teaching, and became the Head of a Department.

National regulations had ensured that facilities on the maternity wards—11 and 14—were good. But ward 7, her gynaecology ward, and ward 13 her antenatal ward, needed a great deal done to them. They were open wards, with high ceilings and stoves in the middle for heat. Toilet facilities were limited. There was no provision for students. For her early years from 1949 she did her gynaecology clinic in the side room of ward 7. Many of the patients were even poorer financially than the DRI ones. Maryfield, too, took pregnant women infected with venereal disease—these did not go to the Infirmary. The nearby psychiatric ward brought some patients with mental diseases also. It was a heavy and tough commitment for her. In later years, the developing geriatric unit of Dr Ossie Taylor Brown added its quota of patients.

Her very first visit to her new gynaecology ward found an elderly and outspoken Dundee woman lying in bed with one of her legs encased in a large metal splint—a Thomas' splint. This *was* a surprise. When she enquired, she found that one of the junior staff had inadvertantly pushed the leg during an operation and it had broken through the shaft. The injured lady declared that if she did not walk out of Maryfield, she would sue him and everyone else. But she agreed to have the splint. Every time the unfortunate registrar came into the ward, she hurled abuse at him as only someone from the Maryfield quarter of Dundee could. After four months she walked out. Honour was satisfied, and the registrar took a well-needed holiday.

Another surprise awaited her when she went into the small antenatal ward. She saw a student, the daughter of a friend. 'What are you doing here?' she asked in amazement. 'Having wisdom teeth out' was the reply. Women dental patients were mixed with the antenatals in Ward 13!

Miss Herring recorded her appreciation of the help she received when she went to Maryfield from Mr Douglas Giffen, who was senior registrar there and later became a consultant in DRI. Because Maryfield was thought a lesser hospital, she had a little difficulty in getting house officers and junior registrars initially, compared with her time at the Infirmary. But now she was her own self and her reputation as a complete lady of high moral stature as well as physically tall and commanding soon meant that increasing numbers of new graduates sought 'to work for Miss Herring and not at DRI'. A little of the draw was that the houseman's six months was all taken up with obstetrics and gynaecology—mainly obstetrics—and not just three months of each, as at the professor's unit. But most of the draw was the wonderful kindness she showed everyone. She could criticise. She could be angry. But never, never, was Miss Jean Herring unkind, and never, never, was she cruel or sarcastic to her staff, nurses or medical, or to her patients or even their relatives. In her presence, people became better.

But just sometimes she allowed her humour and a twinkle in her eyes to take down pride, if she thought it needed. Then she could make use of the fact she was a woman in a men's world in a telling way. Once Professor R. B. Hunter was telling her grandly how 'I am asked to see all these allergic hand conditions in the East of Scotland' when she called him in consultation. 'Are you?' asked Miss Herring with a most serious exression. 'How awful it must be for you. You poor thing.'

It was as an obstetrician that she excelled. Her kindness, her total honesty, and her almost innocent manner belied her skill. In the '50s and '60s, she was a skilled applicator of the forceps, and could deliver with determination if the need arose. Her juniors remembered her particularly as she delivered breach presentations—she did this so well also. As the caesarian section became used more often, she carried this out, but her technical skill was such she could complete vaginal deliveries which a surgical obstetrician of the 80's would just not have believed possible—and these with no danger to mother or child.

As a result, she had a huge private practice. 'It became a terrific amount of obstetrics' she confessed. 'There was only Chis, Dr Fairlie, and me'. When Dr Chisholm retired, it became increasingly Miss Herring. She always, with her characteristic smile and kindly way, did her private confinements personally, by day and night.

She was never so keen on gynaecology. By contrast with 'The Madam', who 'operated like a man', Miss Herring limited herself and did not undertake heroic surgery. Sometimes she allowed her carefulness as an operator to restrict herself in abdominal pelvic surgery; she was much happier with repair type operations.

But overall, she moved through her professional life more smoothly than perhaps any of our Tayside doctors. It was impossible not to like Miss Herring. She had in common with all the fact that she did an enormous amount of work in her chosen speciality, and her career spanned the years of limited biochemical and blood transfusion support to the start of monitored obstetrics ('but I wouldn't like it now' she said of the later 80's 'it's too mechanical'). In gynaecology, she recalled patients with cancer of the cervix with radium implanted inside them 'just lying there in the open ward—it was amazing' in the 1930's. She saw the introduction of refined radiotherapy treatments before her retiral in 1969.

Someone as popular and pleasant was a sought-after member of post-graduate travelling clubs. She became a member of the

Women's Visiting Gynaecology Club as early as 1939—and travelled extensively in Europe with them. She thought their visit to Warsaw, in 1972 after her retiral, perhaps the most memorable. She also belonged to the Medical Women's International Federation and went with them to Melbourne after her retiral, when she took a four month world trip. In 1966–1967 she was President of the Forfarshire Medical Society—again an early woman holder of this office.

There have been only two medical women who became Clinical Chiefs in their own right in Tayside. Professor Margaret Fairlie was one. Miss Jean Herring is the other. While the Professor had undoubtedly the spit, it was her younger colleague who had the polish. She was a very perfect gentle knight of that medical speciality which above all others needs the qualities of kindness and clinical skill combined.

William John Mackintosh

William John Mackintosh

MB, ChB(Edin), 1899–1978

The centuries-old route to the north-east of Scotland has names full of history: Queensferry and Earlsferry on either side of the Forth, Ferry-Port-on-Craig and Broughty Ferry on either side of the Tay. Then the route continues to Aberdeen by way of Arbroath, where The Declaration was signed in 1320:

'It is in truth not for glory, nor riches nor honours that we are fighting, but for freedom—for that alone, which no honest man gives up but with life itself'.

Tayport was the southern crossing point of the Tay on this old route, and a small ferry boat did cross throughout each day to Broughty until the outbreak of war in 1939. Wormit, too, was a crossing point from earliest centuries.

Our last doctor worked in these two old towns, and also in the new town of Newport—which developed as a dormitory of Dundee as that city grew to its years of greatest wealth and prestige in the 19th century. The Newport ferry—the 'Fifie' was the new one—plied between there and Dundee centre.

His family came from Inverness. His forebears were tenant farmers at Drumnadrochit from the time of Culloden onwards. At the turn of this century his grandparents made the decision to give up the farm—probably a wise one when the land is looked at today—and his grandfather moved south to Perth to join the

County Constabulary. He later returned to Inverness and died in post as the Inspector of the Society for the Prevention of Cruelty to Children. His father was sanitary inspector for Inverness-shire, as the Highland region should be properly called. He married twice—our Doctor Mackintosh was the older of the two children of his marriage to Annie Dingwall. His father later married Barbara Murdoch, aunt of George Murdoch, Professor of Orthopaedic Surgery at the University of Dundee.

William Mackintosh was educated at Inverness Academy. By 1916 he had acquired enough Highers to be accepted by Edinburgh University to study Medicine, but like the others in these stories he enrolled in the Services—in the Queen's Own Cameron Highlanders. To be enlisted, he falsified his age. After training in Cameron Barracks, then as now in its wonderful situation overlooking the town and the Moray Firth, his deception was discovered, and he was sent to Invergordon for some months before being drafted to France in 1917. Soon he was gassed. Later, wounded in the foot—the man at his side, a step away, being killed by the same discharge—he was captured and sent to a Prisoner-of-War camp in Belgium. About the time of the Armistice he was on a cattle truck *en route* for Germany but jumped out in the dark and made his way, all on his own, to the Allied lines and eventually back to Inverness.

Now it was 1919 and he joined the huge post-war intake at Edinburgh—he had already been given entrance three years earlier. After qualifying in 1924 he went to the Asylum at Inverness, Craig Dunain, as a medical officer for a year—again following the choice of others of our Ten. Next, after this comparatively undemanding spell, he went as assistant at Fort William to Dr Miller. He lived at Spean Bridge for about a year, and here he met and later married his wife. At this date his work was largely taken up with the medical care of the workers constructing the aluminium scheme. The work was hard and 'it rained every day'. So he tried Bury in Lancashire, again as an assistant in general practice for a year. The work in that industrial town was even harder—especially at nights. The Mackintoshes decided to return to rural Scotland and took a practice at Torphins from 1929 till 1934. Then he moved to Tayport to join the practice of Drs Taylor and Ross, and now he was a Tayside doctor. He remained in practice the rest of his working life; like our others, the Tay was his river and Tayport, Newport and Wormit his places of dedicated service.

The older generation of doctors on that side of the river had been rather formal and severe. 'W. J.' Mackintosh was soon known for his cheerful and hearty laugh, and his friendly kindness, as he went around the homes in the '30s. Tayport and to a much lesser extent Wormit were local, very self-sufficient communities, each with a golf course then, boating at Wormit, and industry with a busy harbour in Tayport. Newport by contrast was younger, and its population for the most part worked in Dundee. In all these were retired men who had lived their lives in the Jute trade in India; Tayport had a large element of jute workers, foundry workers, and sawmill workers: Wormit had more farmers and Fife county workers. The practice extended south to Guardbridge, and Dr Mackintosh held a branch surgery for many years in Balmullo. On the north it extended to Gauldry and Balmerino (reaching a boundary with Dr Tullis), Luthrie and Brunton. At first he lived in Tayport and served the southern part; Drs Taylor and Ross mainly looked after the Wormit end.

His life was as full of drama and amusement as those of Drs Graham and Tullis, in those years between the wars. His wartime training came in useful when accompanying the Physician Superintendent of Inverness Asylum to Aviemore after a telephone call by the local doctor saying there was a 'doubtful case of certification' to be carried out. A few hundred yards from Aviemore station they had to take cover while the patient, on top of a haystack, kept firing with a rifle at them and making close psychiatric assessment somewhat difficult. At Torphins an excitable

105

mother brought in her late teenage daughter to the surgery on account of amenhorrhoea and abdominal bloating. A newcomer to the area, the mother told Dr Mackintosh she was convinced the local water was the sole cause of the problem. 'Yes, it may well be the water, but there is a trouty in it' said W. J.

The Tayside practice was in some way one of contrasts. Tayport had the largest working population, with its jute mills, engineering works and foundry. A rather limited number of families had intermarried, and this sometimes produced interesting familial diseases. Maternity cases were common and fraught with danger. In mid-winter he was called to a gipsy camp where they lived in caravans and did not call the doctor until the second stage of labour. It was often necessary to apply the forceps and on one winter's night, to obtain good traction, W. J. had to back through the open caravan door. By the time he had delivered the baby, his back was covered with snow.

As a diagnostician and observer of the natural history of disease he was superb. A young 7 year old boy had frequent attacks of chest infection, and himself made the clinical observation that his sputum became looser and yellowish or green as the disease progressed. He demonstrated this one day to the doctor, and displayed the chamber pot each day afterwards with interested pride. Dr Mackintosh encouraged him in his clinical observations of these pre-antibiotic days, asked to see his chamber pot each day he called. He later explained the pathological process to his young patient. The interest in disease the boy learned then kindled in him the desire to be a doctor himself when he grew up.

Surgery was also different in these days of the 1930's. A teenage boy went to the surgey with a sore swelling in his neck, so big he could not get his collar fastened. Dr Mack put his head under his arm, saying 'we'll soon put that right for you, Tom', and lanced the abscess swiftly with the scalpel in his other hand. The surgery of the child was often that of the kitchen table, when Dr Mack gave the chloroform while the specialist from Dundee guillotined the tonsils and curetted the adenoids. One small boy climbed out of his bed when the doctors had left, and put his tonsils, still on their swab, in a drawer of his chest-of-drawers. They were a prized possession for many months. Dr Mack laughed and laughed in his own delightful way when he heard the story later from the scandalised mother.

But the other surgery was the major, life-threatening variety. In those days patients really were 'rushed' by car to the ferry, then taken on to Dundee. Anaesthesia and surgery were hazardous. Convalescence was prolonged. Infected wounds drained for weeks.

One of W. J. Mackintosh's great abilities was to put the maximum information into the fewest words when referring a patient for specialist opinion. He had this gift in common with Watty Yellowlees. So good was he that Professor Patrick used to select Dr Mack's patients for his double clinics so that he could read out these wonderfully exact, clear, referral letters, written in small, neat handwriting, to the students.

Much of practice involved repeated visiting and symptomatic care. But added to this was his magnetic laugh, his twinkling eyes, his sometimes sharp questioning. As soon as he entered a home, everyone felt better. The pulse and temperature were recorded, the chest auscultated, the advice given, the bottle prescribed—if he thought necessary. Not only did patients feel they were the only person in the world for him as he spoke to them, so did hospital staff and the consultants of the post-war era.

Like others of our Ten, Dr Mack had a reputation greater than he himself realised. A BBC reporter came from Edinburgh at the end of the war—when, like Dr Tullis he did extra service as RMO to the TA battalion of the Black Watch in Dundee and also—unusually—as auxiliary MO for Leuchars Aerodrome—to interview him for a radio programme. Mr George Bruce, the writer of Scots, had the task, as his family had been patients. He asked 'What do you do when you have established the diagnosis?' 'As a rule, nothing' was the reply. 'Just wait for Nature to take its

107

course. In the majority of illnesses I have to do with, that's all that is needed'. Mr Bruce recognized the wisdom of the remark.

One feature of his practice which differed significantly from that of Dr Tullis was the number of private patients he looked after. While all 'paid' before 1948 and the National Health Service, Dr Mack had a large number who could be called truly 'private'. In spite of the huge demands on his time he still managed to go over to Dundee on the 'Fifie', where he would be met by Dr Jean, Mr F. R. Brown or Mr Robb, or Professor Patrick or Professor Alexander, and go to whichever nursing home his patient was in, to assist at the operation, or just to visit. His constitution must have been of the strongest—one man who developed acute pancreatitis, operated upon successfully by Professor Alexander (who alone had been able to diagnose the condition) in Miss Little's Nursing Home, he visited regularly during his six weeks' convalescence. But he never neglected his other patients—his 'panel'—they received the same regular, constant care. Always was his laugh, his shoulders often shaking with fun or a good joke—for he had a wonderful, kindly sense of humour, and his ring on the door always reassured and cheered.

After 1948 the practice with all others entered the NHS era. But 'W. J.' retained a good deal of private work, and this continued to such a degree that he travelled to Dundee two or even three times weekly, with the 8 a.m. ferry, to be picked up by the consultant (as they were now called) at Dundee, driven to Fernbrae, Marbank or Fort House, assist at the operation or give the anaesthetic, and return to a later morning surgery. At this date—the 1950's—Dr Ross was happy to help out by doing the earlier morning surgeries for him. This suited all partners; Dr Ross had very few private patients, and the extra income Dr Mackintosh's patients brought in benefited the whole practice. In 1955 his son, Kenneth, returned from RAMC service as an 'assistant with a view', and the years ahead seemed assured.

But in 1957 events occurred which led to much anguish and the eventual break-up of the practice. Dr Mona Rodger, who was Mona K. Adamson before her marriage, was appointed a part-time *lady* assistant. The other small Tayport practice of Dr Paton was dispersed on his retiral, and more help was needed. She worked in mornings only, and was attached to Dr Ross' Wormit patients. Dr Ross and she formed a relationship which led to tension—alcohol and drugs were involved—Dr Ross' habits led him to neglect patients, and both were often absent together. The upset to patients gave great anguish to Dr Mackintosh and the older Dr Taylor; the practice become polarised. Unpleasantness and attack over several years hurt these two very deeply. 'W. J.' felt a split was the only solution. Dr Rodger was dismissed; Dr Ross resigned—but as he owned one-third of the Tayport premises he insisted on continuing to practise from them—and he went off on his own, entering a new partnership with Dr Rodger—in 1964. Soon Dr Ross died; Dr Rodger later disappeared while on a cruise on the *Canberra*—lost at sea by accident or otherwise. Just before this she had been joined by Dr Angus Fekety; he returned to the main practice in 1970 after her death. Later he left for New South Wales and the old practice was re-constituted.

This sad interlude left its mark on Dr Mackintosh—'old Dr Mackintosh' as he now was, 'young Dr Kenneth' being the next generation. Just after the split he became ill—he had severe nocturia and in 1965 developed heart failure. He stopped smoking, had his heart failure treated, and in 1966 had a prostatectomy operation in Ward 6 DRI by Mr Soutar. He recovered well, and retired in 1967 in better health once again. He died in 1978.

Not all medical practice runs smoothly. Resentment of others' success can lead to grudges and resentment in hospitals. In general practice, where rivalry is unusual, troubles follow different causes. The sequence of events, involving alcohol and drug addiction, was of the greatest seriousness and was an unexpected happening in a small Tayside practice in the happy surroundings of this part of Fife. But they occurred and left their mark.

But 'WJM' left a deeper and longer-lasting mark. Like Dr Tullis, he experienced the happiness and satisfaction of public acclaim at his retirement and deep public sorrow at his death. Those treated by him as children, encouraged and supported as youth, and counselled as adults, will remember his kindness always. The unpleasantnesses he had to suffer brought no advantage to his pursuers; their own unpleasantness rebounded on themselves. 'WJM' did something no other of our doctors did; he established a practice dynasty likely to continue into the next century.